Winslow Homer
Watercolors

Winslow Homer Watercolors

BY DONELSON F. HOOPES

In cooperation with

The Brooklyn Museum, New York

The Metropolitan Museum of Art, New York

Watson-Guptill Publications, New York

First time in paperback, 1976

First published 1969 in the United States by Watson-Guptill Publications,
a division of Billboard Publications, Inc.
1515 Broadway, New York, N.Y. 10036

Library of Congress Catalog Card Number: 70-83753
ISBN 0-8230-2325-7
ISBN 0-8230-2326-5 pbk.

Manufactured in Japan

First Printing, 1969
Second Printing, 1970
Third Printing, 1971
Fourth Printing, 1972
Fifth Printing, 1976

ACKNOWLEDGMENTS

No subsequent study of Winslow Homer can by-pass acknowledging the pioneering work of Lloyd Goodrich, Director Emeritus of The Whitney Museum of American Art and the greatest living authority on the life and work of this preeminent American artist. I owe a debt of gratitude, also, to the thoughtful studies of Homer made by Professor Philip C. Beam, formerly Director of The Bowdoin College Museum of Art; and to the late Albert Ten Eyck Gardner, formerly Associate Curator of American Art, The Metropolitan Museum of Art. My thanks go also to Bradford D. Kelleher, Sales Manager, and Joseph Veach Noble, Vice-Director, The Metropolitan Museum of Art, and to Thomas S. Buechner, Director, The Brooklyn Museum, for their administrative cooperation in producing this first publication relating the collections of these two great museums. To John K. Howat, Associate Curator in Charge of American Paintings and Sculpture, and to Jacob Bean, Curator of Drawings, go my thanks for their assistance with the Homer watercolors in the Metropolitan Museum's collection. To Sylvia Hochfield, Editor of Publications, The Brooklyn Museum, and to Donald Holden, Editor of Watson-Guptill, I am especially grateful for suggesting and sustaining this project. I am also indebted to the staff of Watson-Guptill—principally, to Margit Malmstrom, for her valuable assistance in coordinating the materials relating to this publication, to Judith Levy, for her careful editing of the manuscript, and to Sally Saunders, for her work in checking the color proofs. No author who relies so heavily upon the quality of the initial photography as I have in the present volume can fail to recognize the valuable contribution of Geoffrey Clements, who made all the color transparencies.

D. F. H.

LIST OF ILLUSTRATIONS

1836. Born in Boston, February 24, the son of Charles Savage Homer and Henrietta Maria Benson Homer.

1842. Family moved to Cambridge, Massachusetts.

1854. Winslow Homer entered the lithography shop of J. H. Bufford, in Boston. Served as apprentice.

1857. Left Bufford and became freelance illustrator.

1859. Moved to New York and took a studio on Nassau Street. Made illustrations for *Harper's Weekly* and *Ballou's Pictorial*.

1860. Exhibited at National Academy of Design, New York.

1861. Moved his studio to New York University building, Washington Square. By fall, he was serving as artist-correspondent for *Harper's* in Virginia with the Army of the Potomac. Took first lessons in oil painting from Frédéric Rondel, New York.

1862. Spent the spring in Virginia with the Union Army on the Peninsula Campaign. Painted his first mature work in oil, *The Sharpshooter*, in the fall.

1864. Elected an associate of the National Academy of Design; exhibited at Academy exhibitions.

1865. Elected full Academician, National Academy of Design.

1866. Painted *Prisoners from the Front*, his most successful picture to date, and acclaimed by the critics. Sailed for France in the fall.

1867. Painted in Paris and in Picardy. Returned to the United States in the fall. Exhibited in the International Exposition, Paris.

1868. Resumed career as illustrator in New York. Spent the summer in the White Mountains, New Hampshire. Exhibited his French pictures at the National Academy of Design.

1870. Spent the summer in the Adirondack Mountains, New York. Exhibited eleven paintings at the National Academy, and one watercolor at the American Water Color Society, New York.

1872. Moved his studio to West 10th Street. Painted two versions of *Snap the Whip*. Exhibited five paintings at the National Academy.

1873. Sketched and painted at Gloucester, Massachusetts during June and July.

1874. Spent the month of June in the Adirondacks painting watercolors.

1875. Contributed his final illustration to *Harper's*. Traveled to Virginia. Spent the month of July in York, Maine. First large showing of his watercolors at the American Water Color Society, New York.

1878. Spent the summer in work at Houghton Farm, Mountainville, New York. Exhibited five genre paintings at the Paris Exposition.

1879. Sketched and painted during the summer at West Townsend, Massachusetts. Exhibited twenty-nine watercolors and drawings at the American Water Color Society, New York.

1881. Sailed for England in the spring. Took up residence in Tynemouth and began painting watercolors.

1882. Returned to America from England in November. Exhibited at the Royal Academy, London.

1883. Stayed briefly in New York, thence to Atlantic City for a holiday. Settled at Prout's Neck, Maine, during the summer. Exhibited a group of his Tynemouth watercolors in Boston.

1884. Sailed to the Grand Banks with a fishing fleet and began work on a related subject, *Eight Bells*. Sailed for Nassau, Bahamas, in December.

1885. Spent the winter in Nassau and Cuba.

1886. Spent the month of January in Florida. Returned to Prout's Neck in March to paint *Lost on the Grand Banks* and *Undertow*.

1889. Spent the summer and fall in the Adirondacks, painting many watercolors. This was the first year that he declined to send paintings to the National Academy exhibitions. He did not resume this association until 1906.

1890. Traveled to Florida for the winter. Exhibited a group of his Adirondack watercolors in Boston. Thomas B. Clarke began acquiring his paintings.

1891. Returned to the Adirondacks for the summer and fall. Repeated pattern the following year.

1893. Exhibited fifteen pictures at the Columbian Exposition in Chicago; awarded gold medal for *A Great Gale*. Exhibited *The Fox Hunt*, Philadelphia.

1894. Spent the month of June in the Adirondacks; then returned to Prout's Neck, where he painted many watercolors.

1895. Made his first trip to Québec in August and September. At Prout's Neck, he finished *Cannon Rock* and *Northeaster*, two of his most important Maine Coast oils.

1896. Stayed for the whole year at Prout's Neck. Exhibited five paintings at the Carnegie Institute, Pittsburgh; awarded gold medal and purchase prize for *The Wreck*.

1897. Made second trip to Québec during the summer; painted many watercolors.

1898. Sailed for Nassau, Bahamas, in December. Twenty-five of his paintings owned by Thomas B. Clarke exhibited at the Union League Club, New York.

1899. Spent the months of January and February in Nassau. Returned to Prout's Neck to begin *The Gulf Stream*. Sailed for Bermuda in December.

1900. Went to the Adirondacks for the month of June. Exhibited four paintings at the Paris Exposition; was awarded a gold medal for *Summer Night*, which was bought by the French Government.

1902. Returned to Québec for the last time; produced many watercolors.

1903. Went to Florida in December; stayed there until February of the next year. Concentrated upon painting watercolors.

1905. Completed his last dated watercolor, *Diamond Shoal*. Went to Atlantic City for his health.

1906. Became ill and was unable to work for quite a long period.

1908. Suffered paralytic stroke in May. Returned to the Adirondacks for the last time.

1909. Last oil, *Driftwood*, completed in November.

1910. Died at Prout's Neck on September 29.

SELECTED BIBLIOGRAPHY

Beam, Philip C. *Winslow Homer at Prout's Neck*. Boston and Toronto: Little, Brown and Company, 1966.

Cox, Kenyon. *Winslow Homer*. New York: Privately Printed, 1914.

Downes, William Howe. *The Life and Works of Winslow Homer*. Boston: Houghton Mifflin Company, 1911.

Gallatin, A. E. *American Water-Colourists*. New York: E. P. Dutton and Company, 1922.

Gardner, Albert Ten Eyck. *Winslow Homer, American Artist: His World and His Work*. New York: Clarkson N. Potter, 1961.

Goodrich, Lloyd. *American Watercolor and Winslow Homer*. Minneapolis: The Walker Art Center, 1945.

Goodrich, Lloyd. *Winslow Homer*. New York: The Whitney Museum of American Art and The Macmillan Company, 1944.

Goodrich, Lloyd. *Winslow Homer*. New York: George Braziller, Inc., 1959.

Hathaway, Calvin S. "Drawings by Winslow Homer in the Museum's Collection," *Chronicle of the Museum for the Arts of Decoration of Cooper Union* (New York), April, 1936.

Ingalls, Hunter. "Elements in the Development of Winslow Homer," *Art Journal* XXIV: 1 (Fall), 1964.

Mather, Frank Jewett, Jr. "The Art of Winslow Homer," *Nation* (New York), March 2, 1911.

Metropolitan Museum of Art. *Winslow Homer Memorial Exhibition*. New York: February, 1911.

Pope, Arthur. "Water-colours by Winslow Homer," *Fogg Art Museum Notes* (Cambridge), June, 1926.

Pousette-Dart, Nathaniel. *Winslow Homer*. New York: Frederick A. Stokes Company, 1923.

Saint-Gaudens, Homer. *Winslow Homer Centenary Exhibition: 1836-1936*. Pittsburgh: Carnegie Institute, 1936.

Watson, Forbes. *Winslow Homer*. New York: Crown Publishers, 1942.

Wright, Willard H. "Modern American Painters—and Winslow Homer," *Forum* (New York), December, 1915.

WINSLOW HOMER WATERCOLORS

In 1908, two years before his death, Winslow Homer was asked by his brother Arthur to make a complete list of his works. The artist, in characteristic fashion, replied testily that he would not do this. Pressed by the argument that if he did not make the list no one would know the full extent of his work after he was "gone," Homer replied, "After I am dead, I shan't care." But a large following of enthusiastic collectors and critics cared enough to make Homer the most widely acclaimed American artist of his day. Indeed, during the last thirty years of his life, Homer enjoyed a renown that few other American artists have ever known. And this adulation came to him at the time of his life when, through personal habit, he was given to periods of isolation from the rest of humanity at Prout's Neck, Maine, disdaining the recognition and praise that were being showered upon him. For Homer possessed those qualities of mind and spirit that indelibly marked him as a Yankee—he was innately resourceful, self-contained, and **indomitable.** His disposition in old age matched the quality of the subject matter he painted: he was intensely defiant, yet strangely attuned to the natural elements he sought in his art. Nearing the end of his long and prolific career, he wrote from Prout's Neck with moving eloquence, "All is lovely outside my house and inside of my house and myself."

Winslow Homer was born in Boston on February 24, 1836. On both sides, his family was descended from old New England stock. His father, Charles Savage Homer, Sr., was the scion of a family long engaged in mercantile pursuits, having made a modest fortune in the shipping trade. Homer grew up in Cambridge, which was then a small community in the countryside beyond Boston. It has been suggested that Homer's essential rapport with nature had, as its basis, the memories of a pleasant childhood spent in the activities of this pastoral existence. His mother, Henrietta Maria Benson, herself a watercolorist of no mean ability, probably contributed as much to Homer's future interests as any discernible influence. She was more than one of those competent lady watercolorists who were products of polite nineteenth century "female seminaries," where an aptitude for dabbling in watercolor was always to be indulged for refinement's sake. Homer's two brothers, Arthur and Charles Savage, Jr., although never artists themselves, in later years always evidenced a definite understanding of their artist brother's ambitions and found his chosen profession meritorious.

When he was about nineteen, Homer was apprenticed to a commercial lithographic printing house in Boston, owned by a family friend, John H. Bufford. His brother Charles alone went to college, for the family's fortunes were low in the years following the elder Homer's disastrous speculation in California gold fields. Winslow entered Bufford's willingly (he had always been interested in drawing), even though the terms of his indenture were hard: in those days, apprenticeship was a privilege for which the student paid. After the first year,

Homer received $5 per week. He had begun his duties at Bufford's producing covers for popular sheet music, but he was transferred to much more demanding work when it was discovered that he had an unusual facility for drawing. But the hours were long—ten hours a day—and the work was arduous without offering any sense of personal gain. In later years, Homer looked upon his time at Bufford's as one of unmitigated drudgery, vowing never again to work for another man.

From his twentieth year onward, Homer was his own man. He cherished his personal freedom as much as he loved the outdoors. In 1857, he quit Bufford's and struck out on his own, taking a studio in the Ballou's Publishing House building on Winter Street, in Boston. Eventually, in June of that year, he obtained an assignment for *Ballou's Pictorial* to produce a portrait in line from a photograph, suitable for conversion into a wood block illustration. That commission was a small beginning, but a promising one. In August, a Homer illustration of a football match at Harvard appeared in the newly established *Harper's Weekly*.

To look at what his contemporaries were doing is to see that Homer, some technical crudities aside, was seeing his world with fresh eyes. That fact is evident almost from the first illustration he produced. Whether they were scenes of families ice-skating in Central Park (he had moved to New York in the Autumn of 1859), or fashionable citizens of Newport taking their ease on the beach, Homer unfailingly gave us life without the sentimental treacle that so often coated the illustration of the period.

As an artist-reporter, he was active in the Civil War, recording the sights of army life for the pages of *Harper's*. In many respects, this experience matured him; and perhaps it is fair to say that because of it, he grew in stature as an artist. Up to this time, his concern was to portray the pleasant ways of well-bred urban life. But with the coming of war, his attention was directed toward the turbulent events that dominated the passions and concerns of the United States for four long years. In 1862, Homer followed McClellan's Army of the Potomac on the Peninsula Campaign, and made many drawings at the Seige of Yorktown.

All of his large war illustrations appearing in *Harper's* were composed in New York after his return. A comparison between the sketches—many of them preserved in the collections of the Cooper-Hewitt Museum in New York—and the finished illustrations reveal that the supple and forceful line of the former was usually made stiff and somewhat awkward in translation. Such discrepancies were often the result of the immoderate hand of the wood block carver, since Homer is not known to have actually executed any of his own designs.

Homer was an authentic, self-taught artist. At no time in his career did he receive any sustained formal instruction in any of the branches of art he successfully practiced. Not since John Singleton Copley had America produced such an innately gifted artist. Although his early drawings of the human figure may be criticized for certain crudities, his eye was awake to nuances of composition and characterization. His native Yankee resoluteness did not permit him to be intimidated by thoughts of caution: what he did not know, he learned by sheer application. In about 1862, he resolved to paint in oils and set about with dispatch the business of learning the rudiments of the technique. From his teacher, a French artist living in New York, Homer took only four lessons before launching out on his own.

His first subjects in oil, taken from sketches he had made at the front, are noteworthy for their sober appraisal of the soldier's life. He exhibited two of his canvases at the 1863 exhibition of the National Academy of Design, where the art critic for his employer's magazine, *Harper's*, found (perhaps with natural partiality) that the artist did not strain for effects, and that his pictures carried no taint of sentimentality, but were notable for their "hearty, homely actuality."

Homer, in effect, had established himself as an important painter in the first year of his work in the oil technique. The suggestion is, of course, that all the years Homer had spent learning how to draw and how to seize upon telling pictorial devices enabled him to blossom spontaneously as a painter. Three years later, he produced his most famous war subject, *Prisoners from the Front* (Metropolitan Museum of Art). When shown at the National Academy of Design, it was hailed as the most important single painting of the war; Homer was made instantly famous. In contrast to the usual salon painting, this picture displayed a realism taken to new heights. *Prisoners from the Front* offered a view, devoid of pictorial clichés, into the bitterness of defeat and the confrontation of captive and captor. The eminent mid-century historian of American art, Henry T. Tuckerman, lauded it, and the picture was immediately acquired by the prominent New York collector John Taylor Johnston. This was meteoric progress indeed.

Of all the great American artists, Homer alone gave no ground to European fashions and influences. His art truly represented the "native school" at its best—a school that relied upon the stimuli of the American experience and gave it the unmistakable stamp of the realist position. Until the advent of its conjunction in recent years with the international style, American art was at its best when dealing with the verities of objective realism. Copley lost his purity of vision to European fashion, and even Thomas Cole's art strained under the weight of old world nostalgia.

Homer's first exposure to Europe came the year after he painted *Prisoners from the Front*. He spent some ten months in Paris—at the very moment when Manet and Courbet were making the bastions of academic conservatism shake with their own unorthodox approaches to realism. Homer, ever the taciturn New Englander, seems to have allowed the heady atmosphere of Paris to sweep over him, to have enjoyed life there without being caught up in the frenzy. He painted as many pictures in the Picardy countryside as he made in Paris, and returned to America barely changed by it all.

Albert Ten Eyck Gardner saw subtle evidences of a Japanese influence in the pictures that followed Homer's exposure to French taste, arguing that so sensitive an eye as his could not fail to be swayed by the same enthusiasm for the pictorial novelties of the Japanese print that was sweeping the *avant-garde* circles of Paris. Perhaps this happened to Homer; but if so, the Japanese influence manifested itself in very subtle ways. Except in certain illustrations for *Harper's* made upon his return from Paris, Homer's presumed recognition of *Ukiyo-e* print compositions is difficult to detect. Homer's approach to art avoided reliance upon lessons from the masters. Similarly, while he also observed what was going on in his own time, he saw no need to borrow manners and styles. He knew what he didn't like: "I wouldn't go across the street to see a Bouguereau. His pictures look false . . . waxy and artificial." The high degree of academic finish, the literary content, and the lack of vitality and animation that so often corrupted academic pictures were anathema to him.

And so, after ten months in Europe, Homer returned to America to resume his former life. In his subsequent work for *Harper's* there was no perceptible influence from this experience. However, as he painted, new dimensions of his talent gradually unfolded. Homer's biographer and the greatest scholar of his work, Lloyd Goodrich, has seen in the landscape and genre pictures of 1868 a "gayer and more fashionable note that may have reflected his French experience." The White Mountain views and the beach scenes of Long Branch, New Jersey, moreover, display a new awareness of sunlight and atmosphere. The light in pictures painted in the studio, usually dominated by a single direction, lacks the quality of light found in nature. The French painters of that era were just beginning to experiment with *plein air* effects, obtainable only by direct observation of nature. No doubt Homer had observed this difference in the quality of light long before his European trip. Gardner has also suggested that Homer may have seen portfolios of watercolors by English artists, as well. Watercolor, essentially a medium of transparent color, lends itself admirably to techniques that quickly capture the effect of brilliant sunlight. However, Homer was not to take up this new medium until the Spring of 1873 when, seeing an exhibition of English watercolors at the National Academy of Design, he may have been reminded of the unique properties of the medium.

The decade of the 70's saw Homer engrossed in portraying the life of the American farmer and mountaineer. It is interesting to contemplate the differences in temperament between Homer and contemporary artists like Eastman Johnson, who were busily engaged with subject matter of an entirely different order: affluent New Yorkers at home. Although Homer lived in New York and kept a studio, first in the old New York University building on Washington Square, and later in the Tenth Street Studios, he gives little indication in his paintings of having been influenced by city life. His interests lay decidedly with people enjoying the outdoors. The pictures of fashionably dressed ladies of Long Branch and the colorful scenes of polite society enjoying such pleasant pastimes as lawn croquet that had been his concern of the late 60's, gradually gave way to contemplation of simpler folk.

Though a decided penchant for depicting stolid country people took over, Homer never descended to the picturesque. His farmers and country boys are not sentimental characterizations, but robust, believable portraits of American rural life. While artists like John G. Brown were providing an eager market with versions of lovable urchins performing stock roles as shoe shine boys and match sellers, Homer, by contrast, saw no merit in such popular folklore; he was concerned with reality in the fullest sense of the word.

If most genre painters were giving a mythical account of life in the cities, this distortion was nothing compared with the stereotyped conception they had of Negro plantation life. Even the warm characterizations of William S. Mount are laden with the white man's mythology of the Negro as a happy, singing, essentially simple soul. In 1875, Homer returned to Petersburg, Virginia, and began a series of paintings of the Negro that remain today as authentic, feeling accounts of what plantation life was actually like. More importantly, he treated each of his subjects as individually as he had portrayed the whites who lived on farms in New York State. Again, one must acknowledge the unusual objectivity of his vision; but one must also note the artist's involvement with the warm humanity of his subjects. Homer's social detachment was complemented by his instinctive desire to create a vision of reality; and these paintings, with their deep and opulent harmonies, are among the richest statements of his career.

A series of watercolors, made at Gloucester, Massachusetts, in the summer of 1873, marked Homer's first sustained efforts in this medium. Somewhat dry and granular when compared with his later work, they indicate a certain hesitancy in adjusting to this demanding technique. He persisted, though, and almost as quickly as he had mastered oil painting, Homer overcame the tentative quality of his first Gloucester watercolors in studies made the following year in the Adirondacks. In looking at these early watercolors, it becomes apparent that Homer usually attacked a problem with assurance; the compositions are rarely anything but the most carefully balanced arrangements. The eye never strays beyond the center of interest except as an excursion, and then is made to return to the principal subject. People are the center of his world during the 70's and 80's. Although

Homer never had formal instruction in drawing the human figure, there is no suggestion of awkwardness in his treatment of it. However, he manages to convey their human quality through the setting, never through recourse to facial expression or exaggerated gesture.

By the end of the 70s, Homer had come to the conclusion of his career as an illustrator. In 1875, already deeply committed to painting, he contributed his last drawing to *Harper's*. His successes at the National Academy of Design annual exhibitions (by 1875 he had been a full Academician for ten years) assured him that his career was taking the right course.

Homer's personality had never been very outgoing. He seemed to prefer the companionship of simple rural people, a few close artist associates, and his immediate family. If this inordinately reserved man knew romance, the experience was probably an early one—and a deep disappointment from which he never recovered. His only excursion into the clubby world of men occurred in 1877, in New York. Homer had been one of the founding members of The Tile Club, along with William M.Chase, Edwin A. Abbey, and J. Alden Weir.

His resignation, ten years later, from this convivial association marks Homer's increasing isolation from the society of men, and coincides in his painting with subjects imbued with a mood of loneliness. Certainly, his remove to the bleak Northumberland coast in the spring of 1881 marked as much of a dramatic break in his art as it did in his life. There, where England's coast meets the North Sea, Homer settled down in a small fishing village, where he lived by himself. Except possibly for a return to the United States in the winter of 1881-82, he remained in this forlorn environment for a year.

His choice of subject matter seems related to his presumed recent affair of the heart. The single dominant note in this year of work was the theme of the women of Tynemouth. Both the oils and the watercolors are heavy with the somber attitudes of his subjects. Indeed, in such a fishing community, the women who waited for their men to return from the sea must have been the most conspicuous and constant feature. However, Homer's vision of this place shows no relief from the constant vigil borne by these brave and stalwart women; no celebration of homecoming is recorded, only the constant attitudes of expectation. Absent also from the Tynemouth subjects is the glowing American sun, and an atmosphere of the joyous felicity of nature.

In some of the larger oils, Homer achieved a kind of *Salon* presence in his rather staged groupings of valiant and obdurate women. One is reminded of the work of Jules Breton, who was almost exactly Homer's contemporary. The suggestion is strong in these Tynemouth paintings that Homer was endeavoring to add seriousness and weight to his subject matter— qualities that had not been especially pertinent to his previous statements, where the optimistic quality of American life had overcome all other considerations.

Tynemouth must be regarded as a watershed in Homer's life, for it was there that he grew accustomed to the self-imposed isolation that was to dominate his way of life thereafter. Returning to America in November, 1882, he went to live at Prout's Neck, Maine the following summer. With the termination of his career as an illustrator, Homer found no compelling reason to remain in New York. Exhibitions of his paintings at the National Academy of Design or at his dealer's gallery in New York could be arranged from his Maine retreat. Since the summer of 1880, he had also occasionally exhibited at Doll and Richard's Gallery in Boston. Although he was not receiving the impressive sums for pictures that came to him in later years, this combined exposure of his art to the world seemed sufficient. He averaged fifty dollars a watercolor during his first showing of the Gloucester series in Boston.

But if Homer experienced certain financial discomforts, the record does not much indicate that they altered or influenced his way of life. Indeed, the recluse of Prout's Neck had housed himself in a former carriage barn belonging to his brother Charles. Homer converted the ground floor into a combination studio and living room. Although in the 1880s Prout's Neck was only a small fishing community, its isolation was more apparent than real, for water surrounded three sides of the small promontory upon which the Homer cottages stood. Even so, Homer moved the former carriage barn closer to the eastern cliffs in order to put more distance between himself and the nearest human habitation. On stormy days, the spray of the open Atlantic crashing on the slanting stone ledges was nearly thrown upon the studio itself. In this raw environment, Homer was to thrive for twenty-seven years.

During this period of his life, Homer produced a series of his most impressive canvases. Commencing with his celebrated *The Life Line* of 1884 (Philadelphia Museum of Art), and concluding with *The Gulf Stream* of 1899 (The Metropolitan Museum of Art), Homer concentrated on painting many variations on a single theme—the struggle of men against the sea. From his vantage point on the rocks at Prout's Neck, he actually witnessed wrecks at sea and ships foundering on the offshore islands; and he knew intimately the wrath and the mystery of the sea. During his first years at Prout's Neck, he probably made a voyage aboard a fishing vessel, learning at even closer hand the terrors that awaited those who ventured upon the sea for their livelihood. Many of his large exhibition canvases lay particular stress upon the theme of this seemingly uneven contest of fishermen, alone in their small dories on the ominously undulating ocean.

As in his previous statements from the sunny days in the Adirondacks, Homer brought no sentimentality to his subjects. Just as his Tynemouth fishermen's wives bravely endured, so did his Maine subjects enter into the contest with nature as part of some grand scheme of life. He chose titles such as *Lost on the Grand Banks* and *The Fog Warning*, more to identify each subject than to suggest unnecessary literary ideas; for these paintings could be understood without the support of words.

The impression Homer gave of himself to the world outside privileged visitors to his lonely studio at Prout's Neck, or to the circle of his immediate family, was one of fierce independence, ill-humor, and general misanthropy. Certainly, the powerful and solemn themes of his paintings from the 80s and 90s tend to reinforce the legendary reputation that grew up around him, and which—for very good reasons—Homer tended to encourage. Philip C. Beam, in his *Winslow Homer at Prout's Neck*, published detailed information concerning Homer's private associations which indicate that Homer had two natures. While he was working or thinking about some problem related to a painting, he was quite loath to be interrupted and, in fact, did actively discourage casual visitors to his studio.

As his fame grew and as Prout's Neck developed as a resort community, there were, of course, an increasing number of curious "summer people" who wanted to see the great man *in situ*. To discourage the timorous lady watercolorists, he posted a sign on the path to his studio: SNAKES! MICE! The resolute intruder who was not deterred by this device met a stern rebuff at the door. Homer, an orderly man in his personal habits, perhaps regarded interruptions of his working hours as the worst form of imposition that could be made upon his time. However, as Professor Beam abundantly documents, Homer could be a model of courtly charm and infinite kindness "off-duty."

But the most telling proof of Homer's warmer nature is to be found in the glorious watercolors of the last twenty-five years of his life. They present such a departure from the character of his Maine oils that they must appear as joyous statements made when the artist, freed from his commitment to paint exhibition pieces, simply relaxed on holiday. Indeed, the great majority of these watercolors were made in the Bahamas, Florida, or the Canadian north woods, where Homer enjoyed a respite from the long Maine winter or pursued his favorite hobby of fishing in the wild rivers of Quebec.

Representing a break with convention, the vast majority of these watercolors served no purpose as preliminary sketches for future reference in his painting. Homer's contemporaries, by contrast, were conditioned to regard watercolor as a sketching medium at best or, less enthusiastically, as something young ladies learned in finishing schools. In the nineteenth century, watercolor was not considered a "serious" means of expression. How much esteem Homer garnered with his first watercolor exhibition in Boston can be seen in the review of the show published in *Nation:* "Mr. Homer goes as far as anyone has ever done in demonstrating the value of watercolors as a serious means of expressing dignified artistic impressions, and does it wholly in his own way." How much further he would go was to be seen in the years following Homer's first trip to the tropics. In December, 1884, he deserted Maine for a two-month vacation in Nassau, telling reporters in Boston (where he passed *en route*) that he was going to Bermuda—perhaps to foil any possible chance for unwanted intrusion.

What met his eyes in the Bahamas was entirely new to him. Light was everywhere, bright and full, charging even the deepest shadows with reflected color. At the outset, his awareness of values and their proper adjustment was somewhat thrown off as he transferred his impressions to paper. Many of the first watercolors tend to be flat because the all-pervading light reduced the volumes of the forms he saw. Homer had always practiced his famous preachment about painting a scene exactly as one saw it. Now, however, he had to make a new adjustment to the nearly blinding light of these islands. Moreover, his technique also retained something of the dry quality of the Gloucester watercolors—a certain stiffness that would quickly disappear as he forged on in his resolute way.

Instead of returning directly to the United States after his Bahama holiday, Homer proceeded to Cuba, where he found in the sights of Colonial Havana more substantial thematic material. Also, the beginnings of two important oils—*The Gulf Stream*, and *Searchlight, Harbor Entrance, Santiago de Cuba* (The Metropolitan Museum of Art)—were recorded in both watercolor and pencil studies at this time. Homer selected a large group of these Caribbean watercolors for an exhibition in Boston during the following December; however, he seems to have met with a reception that was marred by a certain confusion on the part of the critics. Those gentlemen had neither anticipated this unexpected departure in his work, nor, ostensibly, did they know how to evaluate it.

One of Homer's most celebrated canvases, *Undertow* (Sterling and Francine Clark Art Institute), was begun in New York after his return; and, as Goodrich points out, its fresh color bears comparison with Homer's Nassau studies in that he had experienced an "eye-cleansing." Nevertheless, this painting of two young women being carried from a dangerous surf by two stalwart lifeguards (actually posed on the roof of his studio building) seems static and not a little wooden. Perhaps this rigid quality is a reflection of Homer's determination to overcome difficulties in rendering the detailed musculature of his figures. One is reminded that he lacked academic training in drawing the human body.

Paintings of subjects in a similar vein, such as *The Life Line* of 1884 (Philadelphia Museum of Art), became immediately popular, and Homer turned to the art of engraving in order to fill the demand for reproductions that he naturally expected. Once again, he was faced with a technical problem: he had never made an etching. His illustrations for *Ballou's* and *Harper's* had been rendered by others—craftsmen long experienced in the art of wood block engraving. But Homer threw himself into this new task with his usual aplomb, seeking advice where he could find it. Almost miraculously, in 1887 he produced a thoroughly competent performance in a reproduction of his well known marine subject, *Eight Bells*. Goodrich records that although Homer had begun to have optimistic expectations for commercial printmaking success, the venture proved not to be rewarding to Homer in any respect. The etchings somehow failed to attract the same critical appreciation that his paintings had won. This effort represented about two years of his life, and left Homer somewhat bitter.

In the summer of 1889, he returned to his beloved Adirondacks, making subsequent trips to this mountainous region in the seasons of 1891 and 1892. The beginning of the decade of the 90's seems to have ushered in a new element in the artist's work, for his paintings of lonely Adirondack mountain men have none of the heroic drama that marks his earlier pictures. Rather, there is in these new oils an atmosphere of isolation that pervades his paintings more and more with each passing year. By the end of the decade, he ceased to paint women. Finally, the human element disappeared almost entirely from his oils. Nature alone dominated the themes of his last paintings as Homer became engrossed with its elemental forces. The confrontation of irresistible sea and immovable rock became for him as much a mystery to be explored as man and the sea had been earlier. Such was his life at Prout's Neck that his physical requirements were reduced to the utmost simplicity, and his daily routine of work was tuned to the rising and setting of the sun which, he observed, would not pass "without my notice, and thanks."

Homer believed that he would best be remembered for his watercolors. In the record of American art, his accomplishment stands on a pinnacle of achievement shared only by Sargent's masterly handling of the medium. As early as 1917, when the Carnegie Institute held its double exhibition, these two masters of watercolor were being compared. Their work is eminently different: while Homer's art is rooted in his admiration for nature and its straightforward realism is intensely American, Sargent's work reflects the charm of a more cosmopolitan mind. Both the Metropolitan Museum of Art and the Brooklyn Museum long ago recognized the significance of Homer's work and collected it in depth. The Metropolitan Museum acquired its important Homer oils between 1906 and 1910, when twelve watercolors were also added to the collection. The Brooklyn Museum has only two Homer oil paintings, but exceeds the Metropolitan in its holdings of watercolors. With the addition in 1969 of an early Bahama subject, the Brooklyn Museum's group of watercolors now numbers twenty-one. In 1911, Brooklyn purchased eleven watercolors directly from Homer's brother Charles. Seen together, these two museum collections offer a rich and varied selection from Homer's prolific career. That these watercolors remain fresh and clear to modern eyes is the conclusive testimony to their inherent greatness.

Color Plates

During the summer of 1878, Homer visited a place called Houghton Farm, at Mountainville, New York. This was a pleasant country retreat owned by a business partner of his brother Charles. It was an enormously productive summer for Homer, attested to by the number of works he exhibited the next year at the Water Color Society. One of his prevalent themes is the shepherdess and her flock; for a brief time, Homer seems to have been caught in the spell of nostalgia for the eighteenth century, a phenomenon which swept the country in the wake of the Centennial Exposition of 1876. The costume worn by the young girl in *Fresh Air* appears time and again in the 1878 watercolors. Homer brought the costume with him from New York, which suggests that he wished to achieve a greater fidelity to the effects of light and air than could be had in the studio. One of the very rare interviews Homer permitted was given to George W. Sheldon, who published his observations in an issue of the *Art Journal* in 1878. Sheldon followed Homer's career, observing some years later that, ". . . while the theorizers were splitting hairs with their battleaxes, the painter himself stepped into the midst of them, and introduced the American shepherdess. At the sight of the maid, Philosophy herself stood still." Not all of his critics were so sanguine. The erudite Henry James, like so many European-oriented Americans, found it difficult to see any merit in the works of the native school: "Before Mr. Homer's . . . little girls in calico sunbonnets, straddling beneath a cloudless sky upon the national rail fence, the whole effort of the critic is instinctively . . . to double himself up, as it were, so that he can creep into the problem . . . . [Homer] is almost barbarously simple, and, to our eye, he is horribly ugly; but there is neverthless something one likes about him. . . . He has chosen the least pictorial features of the least pictorial range of civilization; he has resolutely treated them as if they *were* pictorial, as if they were every inch as good as Capri or Tangiers; and to reward his audacity, he has incontestably succeeded." Homer, who had spent an active ten months in Paris in 1867, was not unaware of the precedents set by European art. But instead of dreaming about worlds which were foreign to him, he set his hand to recording that which he knew and loved best—the American scene. The "shepherdess" theme proved to be a passing fancy; the subjects which followed—homely farming people and mountaineers—were more substantial to his art. However, the Houghton Farm watercolors strongly intimate the powerful command over the medium that Homer was to demonstrate in later years.

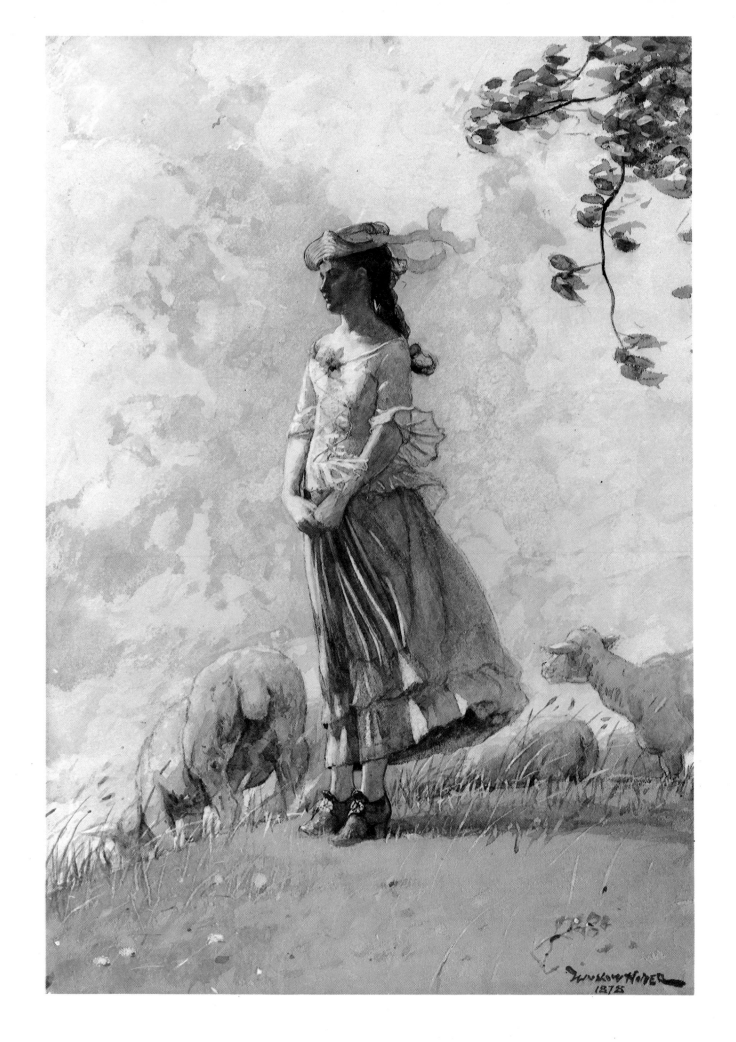

Plate 2

INSIDE THE BAR, TYNEMOUTH, 1883

15¾″ x 28½″ (39.1 x 72.4 cm.)
The Metropolitan Museum of Art
Gift of Louise Ryals Arkell, in memory of
her husband, Bartlett Arkell, 1954

Homer traveled to England in the spring of 1881 and settled down in a small fishing village near Tynemouth, on the Northumberland coast. Here, under the lowering skys of the North Sea, he discovered people whose simple lives seemed to him to take on heroic proportions. The women of this community, particularly, find a special place in his attentions. Gone from them is the sweetness and the prettiness that is reflected in his pictures of American women; rather, they are physically robust, almost manly. *Inside the Bar* shows one of these women, bareheaded, standing resolutely against the force of the wind, which is admirably suggested by her billowing apron. She carries a basket for gathering mussels and, in the slight lee of the rock split in the middle distance, she seems to be defying the elements. Beyond her, a small shallop makes its way to the open seas.

Here, the color scheme is carried out in dull blues and brown, probably closely approximating the actual look of the place. But Homer has relieved the grayness of the composition by placing his strong accent—the woman's red scarf—at the center, reinforcing it with the rich indigo of the skirt. This subject, with its intimations of danger and with its suggestion of the meagre comforts of the life it depicts, never descends to the picturesque or the sentimental. The life that Homer briefly shared with these fishermen seems to have been one of full participation. He lived alone in a small rented cottage, and there existed simply. When the storms of the North Sea ravaged the coast and imperiled fishermen on that sea, Homer must have keenly shared the anxiety of his neighbors ashore. He recorded his impressions and feelings honestly, honoring by his straightforward approach the people whom he respected.

The date 1883 appears on this watercolor along with Homer's signature, which is applied in the heavier, block letters he employed at a later time. There is the possibility, therefore, that this work may have been done after Homer's return to the United States, rather than during the 1881-82 season he spent at Tynemouth. In point of style, the drawing of the figure is clearer and somewhat harder than in works definitely ascribed to Tynemouth.

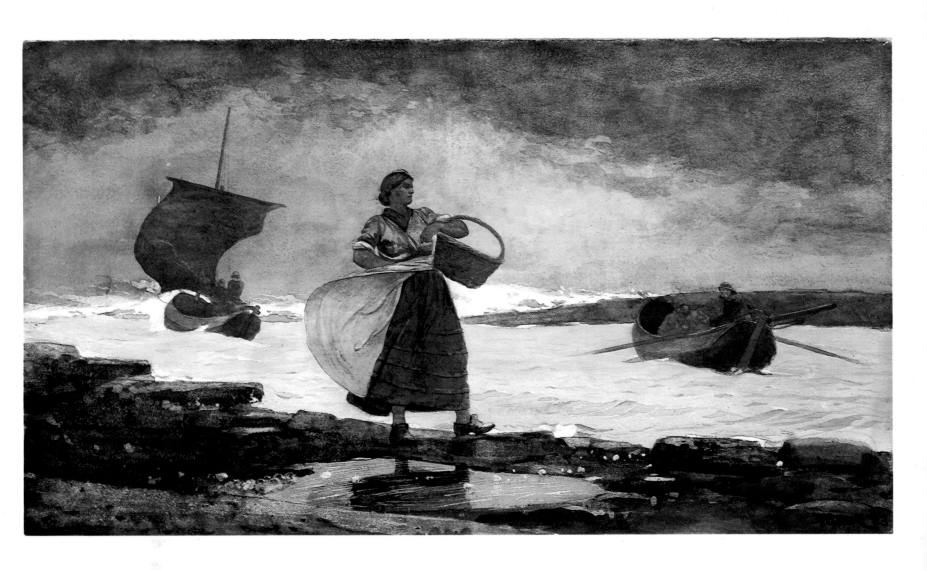

Plate 3

FISHER GIRLS ON THE BEACH, TYNEMOUTH, 1881

13" x 19⅜" (33 x 49.2 cm.)
The Brooklyn Museum
Purchase Fund, 1941

Most of the Tynemouth watercolors show a striking departure in technique from Homer's earlier work in the medium. This damp, chilly, and sunless coast gave him the kind of views that are best caught by applying a series of washes which, superimposed one over another, build toward a dull luminosity. Goodrich notes that Homer's work acquired a more rounded modelling of form, ". . . while new strong sober hues created harmonies of a depth and ripeness he had never attained before."

In the *Fisher Girls on the Beach*, he accomplishes the feat of producing a remarkably colorful picture out of the simplest of combinations—essentially, burnt sienna and blue. The figures of the girls in the foreground are precise without being labored, and the figures and coast in the middle distance are suggested with the utmost ease and economy. The reflections of the figures on the wet sand convey wetness in an understated way that demonstrates Homer's capacity for rendering effects such as these—brilliantly, but without swagger. Kenyon Cox, an American painter who admired Homer and who, with a painter's eye, wrote about him in 1914, observed: "At Tynemouth he learned to envelop his figures in fleecy softness and to place his landscape *in* the sky rather than in front of it . . his new sense of the enveloping atmosphere is a permanent acquisition, without which the creation of his great sea dramas would hardly have been possible." The Tynemouth experience became deeply embedded in him, and all of his subsequent treatments of the theme of the sea bear references to it. As late as 1897, when Homer painted *A Light on the Sea* (The Corcoran Gallery of Art, Washington), there appears the figure of a woman strikingly similar in character to his Northumberland fishermen's wives.

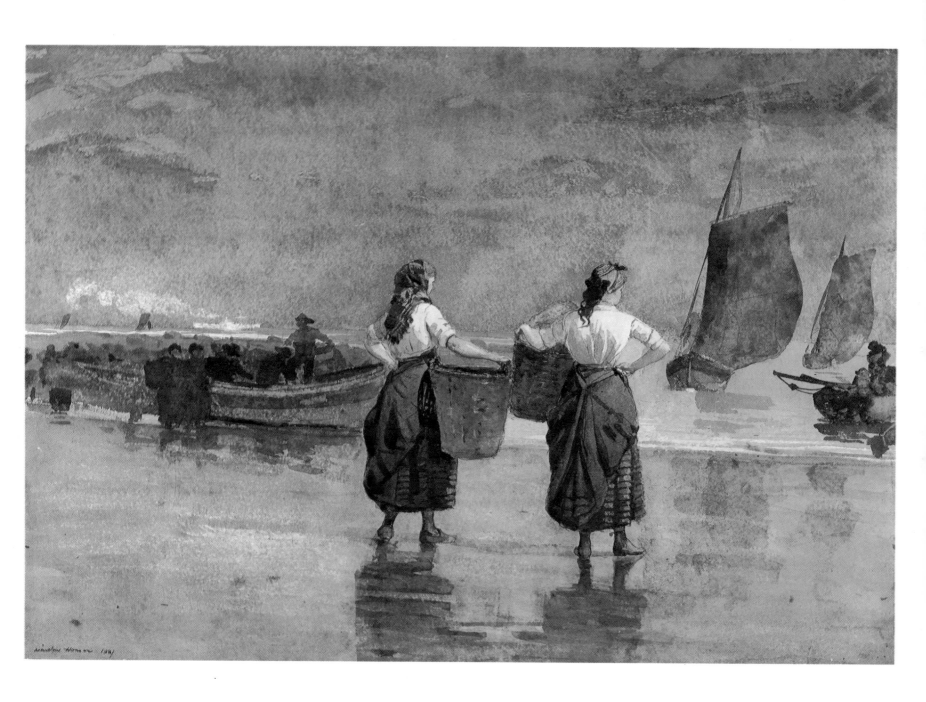

Plate 4

MAINE CLIFFS, 1883

13³/₈'' x 19¹/₈'' (33.9 x 48.6 cm.)
The Brooklyn Museum
Bequest of Sidney B. Curtis in memory of
S. W. Curtis, 1950

Homer returned to the United States in November, 1882, and after a period of work in New York and a brief holiday on the New Jersey shore, settled in Prout's Neck, Maine for the balance of the summer. One may speculate about Homer's seemingly immediate affinity for the rugged Maine coast. Perhaps, after the year spent at Tynemouth, he felt he was no longer suited to city life.

In *Maine Cliffs*, the only indication of human presence is barely discernible in the tiny notations of ships on the horizon. His concern here is for the abstract shapes of the rock ledges and the patterns made upon them by the outgrowths of wild blueberry bushes. The use of color is restrained, but the juxtaposition of rich greens with touches of red accent and the cool blue shadows against the neutral warmth of the rock is ravishing. This isolation of his interest in the study of a magnified fragment of nature, devoid of the human element, is rare in Homer's work at the early part of his career.

This watercolor carries with it the suggestion of an "arrangement" not unlike that element found in European painting under the influence of Japanese taste. Homer's exposure to actual works of Japanese art in the Exposition of Paris in 1867 must be presumed; but whatever residual interest he may have retained is usually thoroughly submerged in his work. On these same cliffs, as his earlier biographer William Howe Downes records, Homer trained the wild juniper bushes to grow in the manner of *bonsai*. On a summer day on the Maine coast, sometimes the fog, drifting in from the sea, will create a thin, pearly vapor in the air that permits the sun to cast distinct shadows; but the light is pale. Homer has suggested such an effect in this watercolor, adding to a subtle sense of mystery by giving us just enough of a glimpse of the distant scrub conifers and horizon to evoke a wanderlust for the world beyond this microcosm.

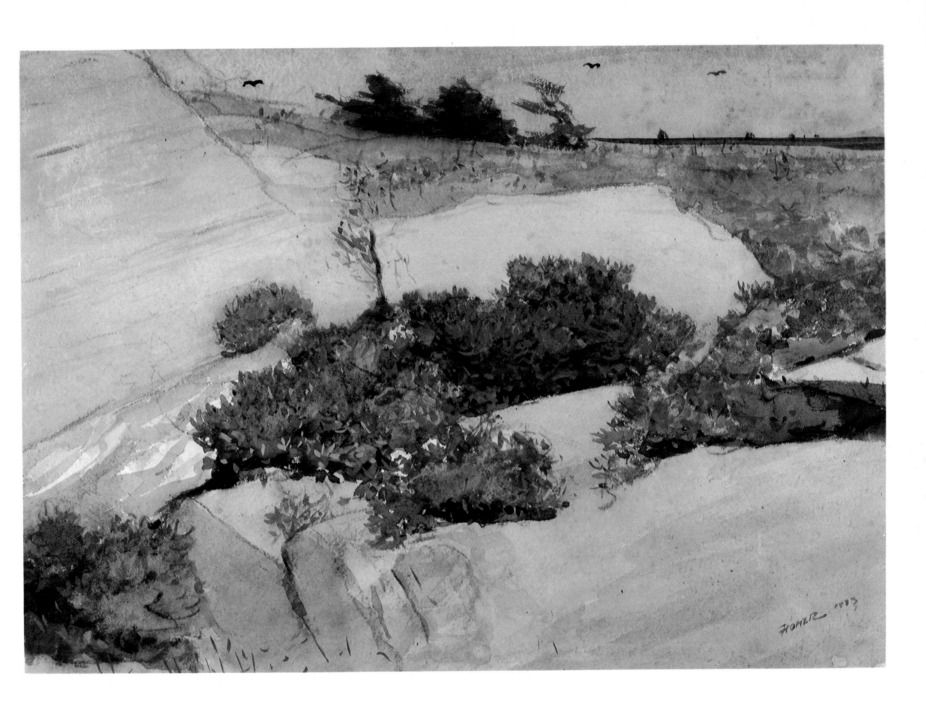

Plate 5

THE NORTHEASTER, 1883

14" x 19¾" (35.5 x 50.2 cm.)
The Brooklyn Museum
Bequest of Sidney B. Curtis in memory of
S. W. Curtis, 1950

Homer's studio, converted to that use from a carriage barn on his brother's property at Prout's Neck, faced the open Atlantic. The artist was given to studying the effects of the sea for long hours, both from the protection of a covered balcony porch on the studio, and from the rocks themselves. Philip C. Beam, who has made an intensive study of all aspects of Homer's life at Prout's Neck, has observed that because of the angle of the ledges to the water there, the effects produced by ground swells breaking upon the shore is particularly impressive: "A fall three-day northeaster . . . will create forty and fifty foot waves, and when they break, the salt spray will fly like solid shot over the tops of the sixty foot cliffs."

In this work we are shown, perhaps, the aftermath of such a storm. Two figures, dressed in tam-o-shanters, observe the surf from a vantage point high on the ledges. Homer's ability to describe the movement of water is nowhere better demonstrated. He has selected a point in time when a breaker is receding toward the ocean, its force spent on the rocks which have reduced it to boiling surface foam. Coming to meet the shore is a new wave, whose ominous force is hinted at by the long curve of its incipient crest. On the horizon, a steam vessel can be dimly perceived as the weather begins to lift. All is bound in a pearly translucence of the most muted color. The suggestion of distance is achieved in delicate washes which, in their subtlety, nearly defy indentification. The range of values is kept at such a consistently high level that, where dark accents do occur (such as in the rocks in the foreground), they are powerful yet economical.

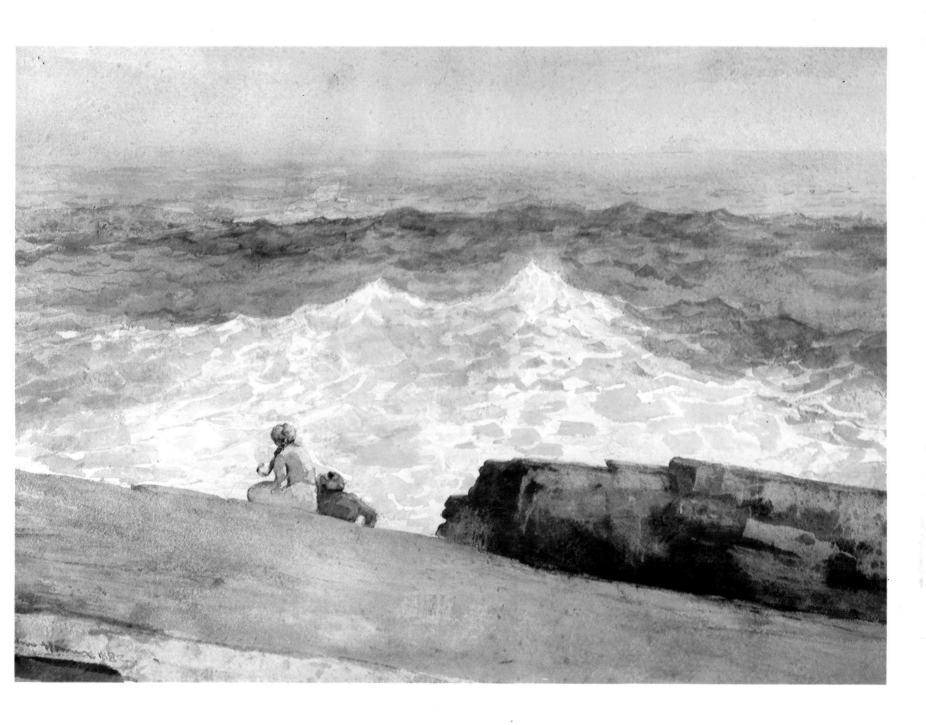

There is probably no stretch of shoreline, no outcropping of rock, or seaward-slanting ledge on the entire promontory at Prout's Neck that Winslow Homer did not know intimately. Downes, describing the artist's life at Prout's wrote: "He knew and loved every part of the cliffs and rocks. A beautiful walk runs along the top of the cliffs from his cottage eastward winding along in front of the unenclosed grounds of the cottages. . . . As one strolls along this path, never out of sight and sound of the sea, there are numerous striking points of view, and it is easy to recognize many of the subjects of Homer's most masterly marine pieces. Here are Cannon Rock, the Spouting Cave, Kettle Cove, Eastern Point, Pulpit Rock. . . ."

In this view, looking northeast toward High Cliff, a small patch of the cove is embraced in a natural window of rock. The atmosphere is laden with mist, and the color is soft and muted. The enclosing device of the rocks provided the artist with a novel theme: in the center of a stationary frame, a constantly shifting and changing area of color and form is perceived as action on a stage where time and movement are always isolated and defined. It is interesting to note that Homer reinforced this idea by enlarging the rock at the upper right, making a more secure enclosure for his captive piece of ocean. Achieving a palpable representation on paper or canvas of the eternally shifting patterns made by the sea is a difficult quest. Some marine painters, like Alfred T. Bricher (Homer's exact contemporary) tried to memorize those patterns. Bricher's method was to stare intently at a forming wave, then look away and try to recreate what he had seen. There is none of this naturalistic precision in Homer's work; his seemingly spontaneous and effortless representations of the sea, in all its infinite variety, were the product of his feeling for it, as much as of his understanding.

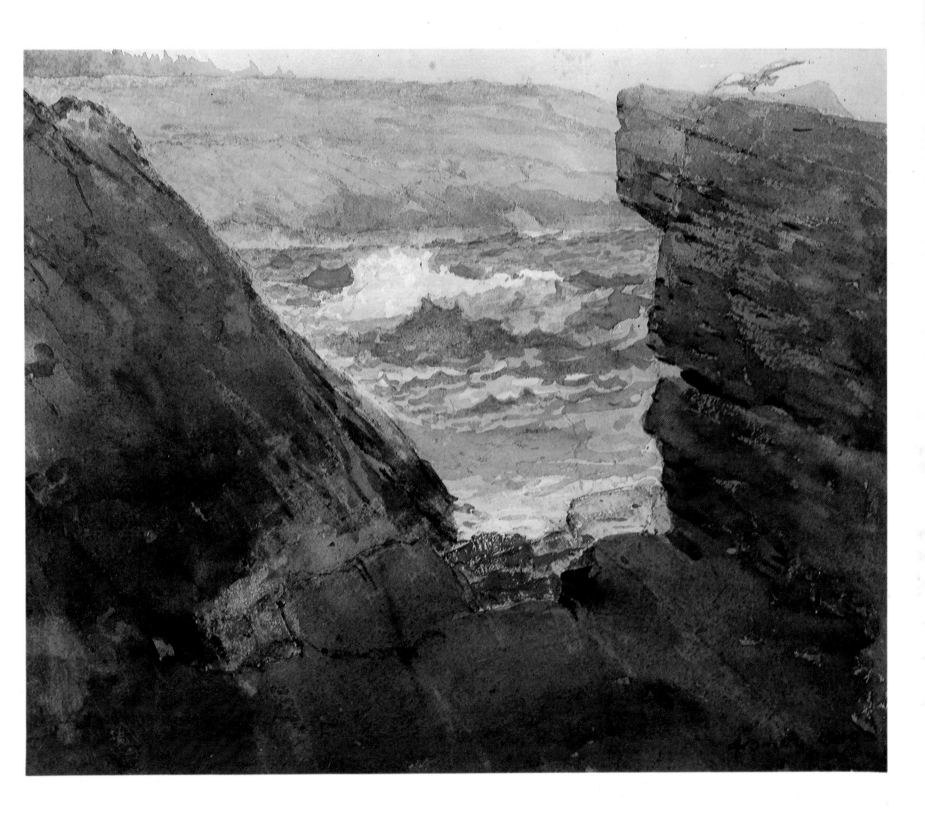

Plate 7

BLOWN AWAY, ca. 1888

10" x 19" (25.7 x 48.3 cm.)
The Brooklyn Museum
Purchase Fund, 1911

In the upper right corner of Homer's oil painting, *Summer Squall* of 1904 (Sterling and Francine Clark Art Institute, Williamstown), there is a poignant detail of a small sailing dory being driven before the wind, out of control and with its sail wildly billowing. This Brooklyn watercolor, made several years before the oil, shows the origin of the *Summer Squall* motif, with certain differences. In the former, the gentle, rolling s-curve, which seems to draw the small craft inexorably onward, bears striking similarities in circumstance—if not in treatment—to the well known Hokusai print, *The Great Wave off Kanagawa*. Both Beam and Gardner have drawn comparisons between the work of Homer and Hokusai. Certainly the occult balance of *Blown Away*—the void on the right balancing, in a negative way, the object on the left—would suggest that Homer was not unconscious of the uses to which the newly-appreciated Japanese master's examples could be put. The Williamstown picture, on the other hand, gives much more animation to the surface of the sea on which the boat rides, bringing the treatment of the distant secondary focal point into harmony with the agitation of the breakers in the foreground.

Blown Away was inspired by an actual incident, according to Beam. One of the local sailors had taken a group of neighbors' children for a short cruise off Prout's Neck when, without warning, the boat was caught in a sudden and violent summer squall. The sailor, who knew the dangers of being thrown up on the lee shore, guided his disabled craft to open water and waited for the storm to subside. All eventually returned safely to land, but the incident left a powerful impression in Homer's mind. *Blown Away*, with its nearly monochromatic tonalities, comes very close to being a "symphony in gray" in the same vein that we have come to consider idiomatic in the work of James Whistler. But perhaps it would be fairer to say that, in Homer's hands, the mood is closer to a tone poem.

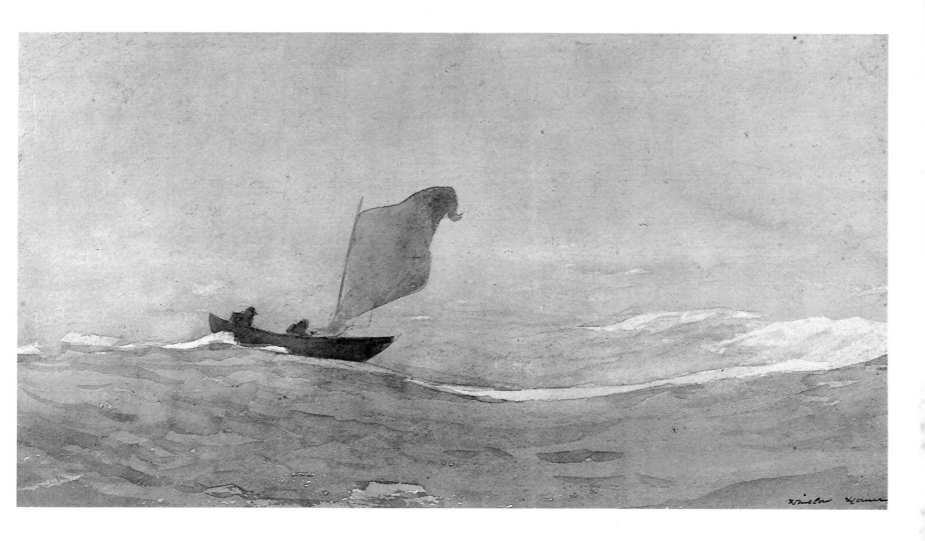

Homer's first trip to the tropics was made in the winter of 1884-85. His first stop was Florida, and from there he took a steamer to Nassau. As his boat crossed into the warmer waters of the Gulf Stream, Homer saw his first shark, and he determined to sketch a specimen upon landing. It can be only imagined with what curiosity he entered this lush, exotic, and often dangerous new world. Everything about these latitudes was new to him, especially the quality of the light. In *On the Way to Market*, the light is all-pervading. Its midday intensity is harsh, tending to flatten the form of the figure, the stone wall, and the trees beyond. The evidence of Homer's pleasure in discovery is to be found in this veritable survey of tropical flora, for represented are the cocoanut palm, the frangipani with its ruby leaves, and orange and grapefruit trees. The native woman, in her calico bandanna, carries a pair of brightly plumed Bantams.

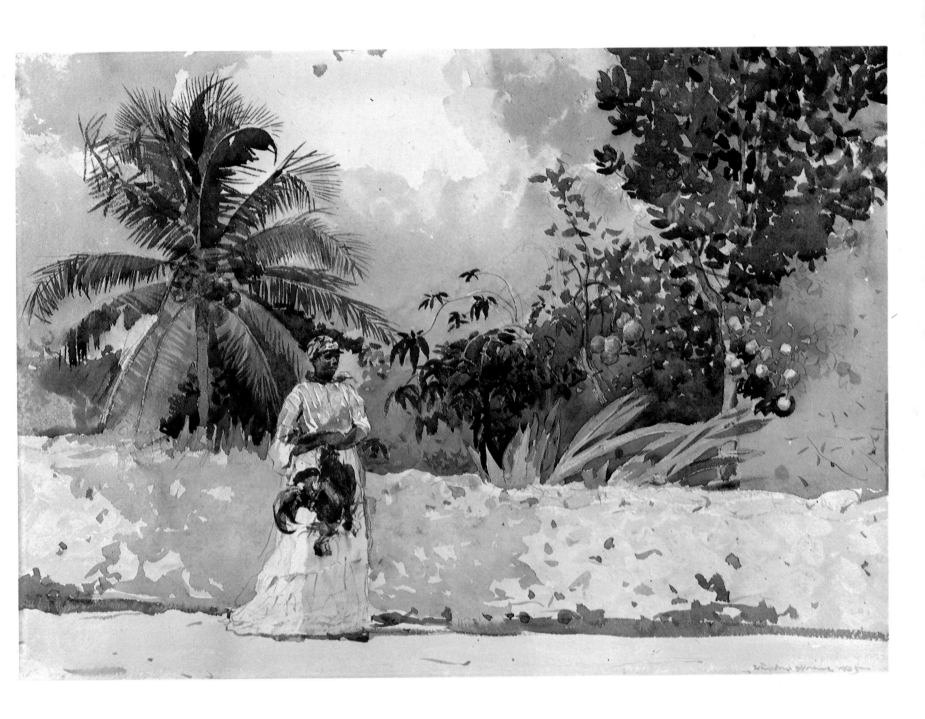

Plate 9

A WALL, NASSAU, 1898

14¾" x 21½" (37.5 x 54.6 cm.)
The Metropolitan Museum of Art
Amelia B. Lazarus Fund, 1910

In 1898, Homer made his second trip to the Bahamas. After an absence of nearly thirteen years, his performance in this watercolor seems curiously close to the technique he first employed there. A certain dryness which is characteristic of his earlier Bahama watercolors prevails. However, the sheet is plainly signed and dated "Dec. 31, 1898/Nassau," which would seem conclusive, unless Homer erred in postdating this work. During the interval between 1885 and 1898, he made two trips to Florida, four to the Adirondacks, and two to Québec province, and on all of these travels, he completed many watercolors. In addition, he was active with the medium at Prout's Neck during various summers. Perhaps the degree of stiffness noted here may be assigned to prosaic subject choice. The gray stone walls of Nassau, with their singular lack of decoration, serve as foils for the highly colorful frangipani and fruit trees in a number of Homer's Bahama watercolors. Yet, in such a deliberate choice, the artist seems to be setting up a challenge for his abilities. To paint a nondescript wall as an important element in a composition demands an enormous assurance. Homer's rival in watercolor, John Singer Sargent, painted similar walls on the Mediterranean island of Corfu at about the same time.

A Wall, Nassau reveals itself slowly, despite its apparent simplicity. It is a study in contrasts, balances, and tensions: the contrast of neutral and bright color; the balance of the doorway's exaggerated off-center position against the dominant emptiness of the wall; and the tension between the doorway and the distant sailboat. But the explosion of the frangipani leaves against the ultramarine sky is a transcendent visual experience.

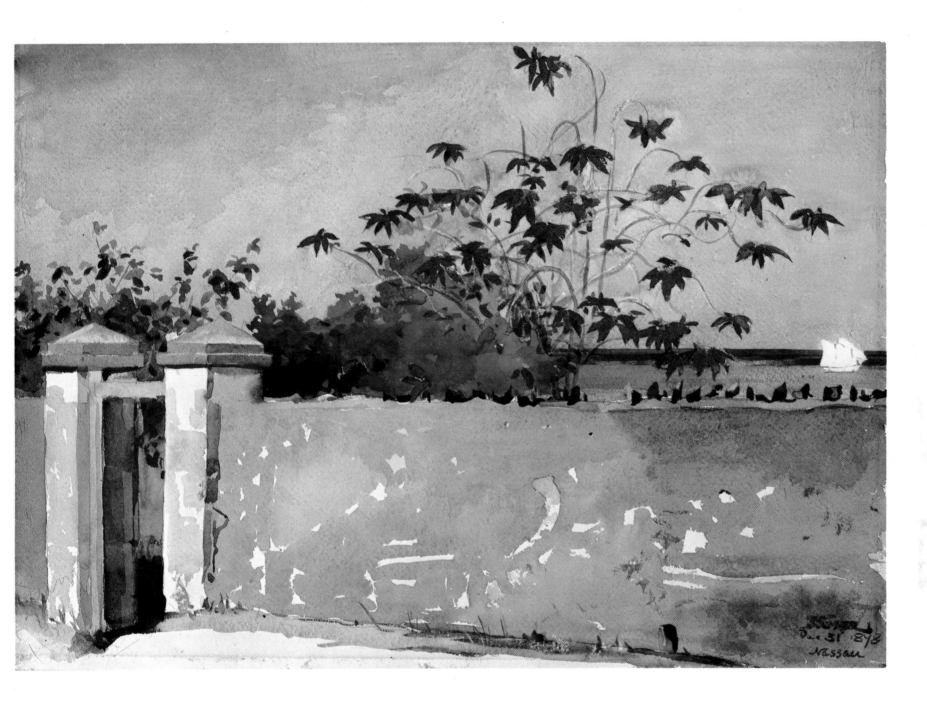

Returning to the Bahamas after so many intervening years, Homer found the experience bracing and joyous. As he wrote to his friend, the collector Thomas B. Clarke, ". . . a most successful winter at Nassau. I found what I wanted and . . . desire to report myself *very well.*" Goodrich points out the suspected streak of paganism that lay dormant in Homer, and which was liberated by this contact with primitive life in these islands. The Negro had a special importance, for as Goodrich remarks, "The superb beauty of the black bodies and the spectacle of this free life in such a setting gave these works, with all their realism, that pagan spirit we call Greek." Few examples of his work can match the intensity of sunlight that Homer captures in *The Turtle Pound,* with its jewel-like reflections in the water and the glowing skins of the figures. Here, particularly, Homer treats his figures as individuals, noting differences in flesh tones and expressions. The man inside the enclosure waits to seize the wildly struggling sea turtle being hoisted by his companion; this ordinarily commonplace activity attains a monumentality in Homer's vision.

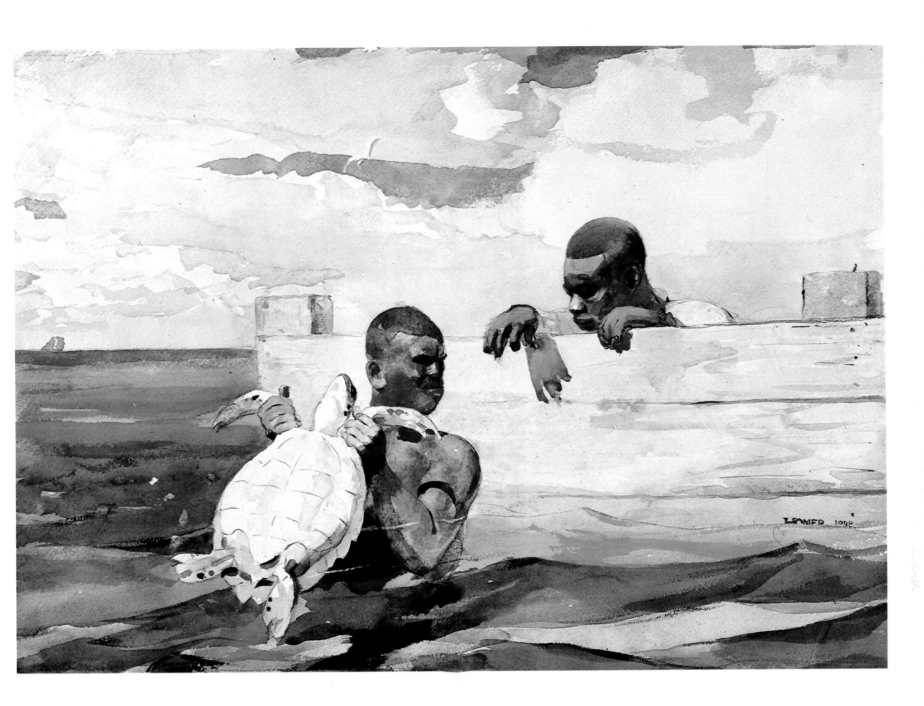

Plate 11

PALM TREE, NASSAU, 1898

23³/₈'' x 15'' (59.4 x 38.5 cm.)
The Metropolitan Museum of Art
Amelia B. Lazarus Fund, 1910

Homer was in his middle sixties when he visited Nassau for the second time. He had been a late blooming artist (by the time he finally found his *métier* at Tynemouth, he was into middle age). How extraordinary, then, seems the outpouring of the Bahama watercolors; they appear in his life's work very like the bursting of some emotional dam. The intense pleasure he shows in the manipulation of the medium, and the visual excitement he sustains in each of these remarkable papers surely speaks of an artist who knew that he had come face to face with a world he could claim as his own province in paint.

The ability of an artist to communicate his emotions about a subject, to transcend time, and to make the experience ever fresh in the senses—all of this is achieved in Homer's pictures of wind-tossed palm trees. Looking at *Palm Tree, Nassau,* one can almost hear the rattling of tattered fronds, while across the channel by the stone lighthouse a red storm signal flag snaps taut in the oncoming breeze. The picture is elegantly and simply composed; but in Homer's watercolors, especially, one is not particularly aware of the mechanics of composition, for their appeal is usually directed at the emotions.

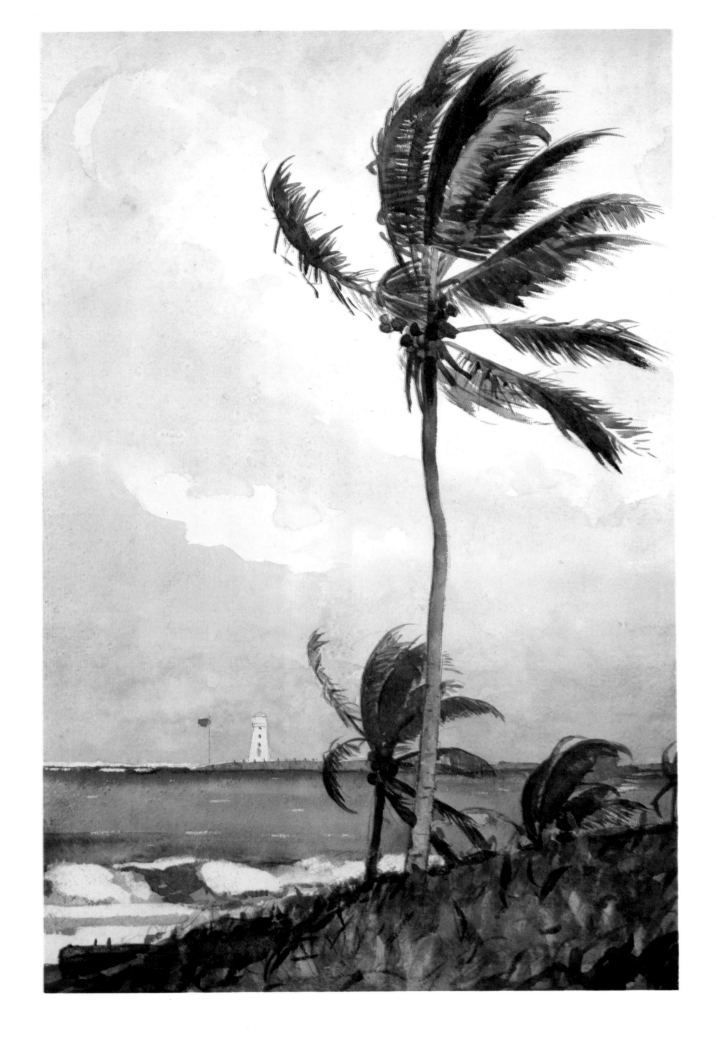

Plate 12

HURRICANE, BAHAMAS, 1898

14½″ x 21″ (36.8 x 53.3 cm)
The Metropolitan Museum of Art
Amelia B. Lazarus Fund, 1910

In old age Homer said to his dealer, Charles R. Henschel of Knoedler's, "You will see, in the future I will live by my watercolors." Surely, if any one of the Bahama subjects were to be pointed out as one Homer "lived by," it would be *Hurricane, Bahamas*. It is a curious picture, at once strangely awkward and yet convincing. One has the impression that it was painted directly from nature, perhaps very quickly during the interval between the gathering of the storm's first clouds and the onset of the torrential winds and rain. There are discrepancies in the drawing that seem purposeful: the palms are indicated with ease and infinite sensitivity, yet the houses seem flat and crude in execution. The flattened perspective of the buildings again offers a reminder of oriental approaches to drawing.

Beam takes the comparison farther in his book by comparing the treatment of the palms to the way a fourteenth century Chinese scholar painted bamboo. Whether or not such comparisons actually reflect Homer's inspiration in this watercolor, the work is, undeniably, one of his most powerful statements. The grouping of low triangles representing the gable ends and roofs of buildings suggest a certain tenacity, as if they were living things huddled and clinging to the earth lest they be swept away in the fury of the storm; while the palms, in spite of their apparent fragility, stand erect, defying the power of the hurricane.

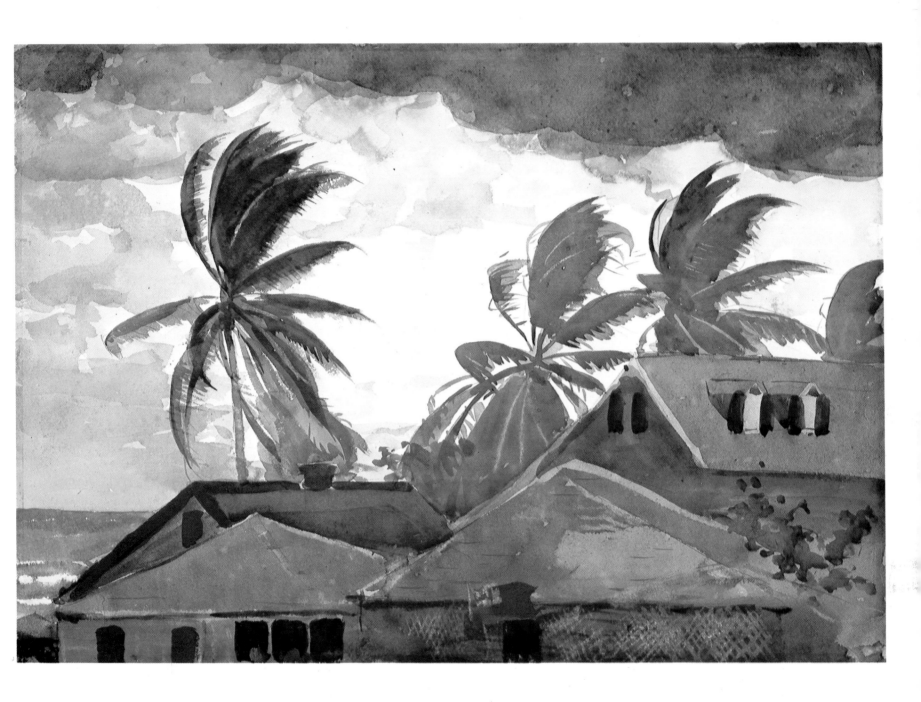

Plate 13

NEGRO CABINS AND PALMS, 1898

14³/₈" x 21" (36.5 x 53.3 cm)
The Brooklyn Museum
Purchase Fund, 1911

This subject originally carried the designation, "Key West," but Homer did not visit Florida during the year which appears inscribed on this paper. The erroneous title came with the picture at the time of its purchase from the artist's brother Charles S. Homer, Jr., who may have assigned it rather than Homer himself, who died a year before the work came into the Brooklyn collection.

This picture is, unquestionably, one of Homer's most assured and facile performances in the watercolor medium. The entire picture is composed of washes of color, almost without benefit of an underlying drawing. The quality of the atmosphere superbly evokes a humid tropical torpor whose stillness presages a storm. Brilliant dots of red, indicating men's shirts, punctuate the dull greens and Indian reds of the scene; the artist's evident enjoyment lies in rewarding the patient eye with such pleasurable surprises.

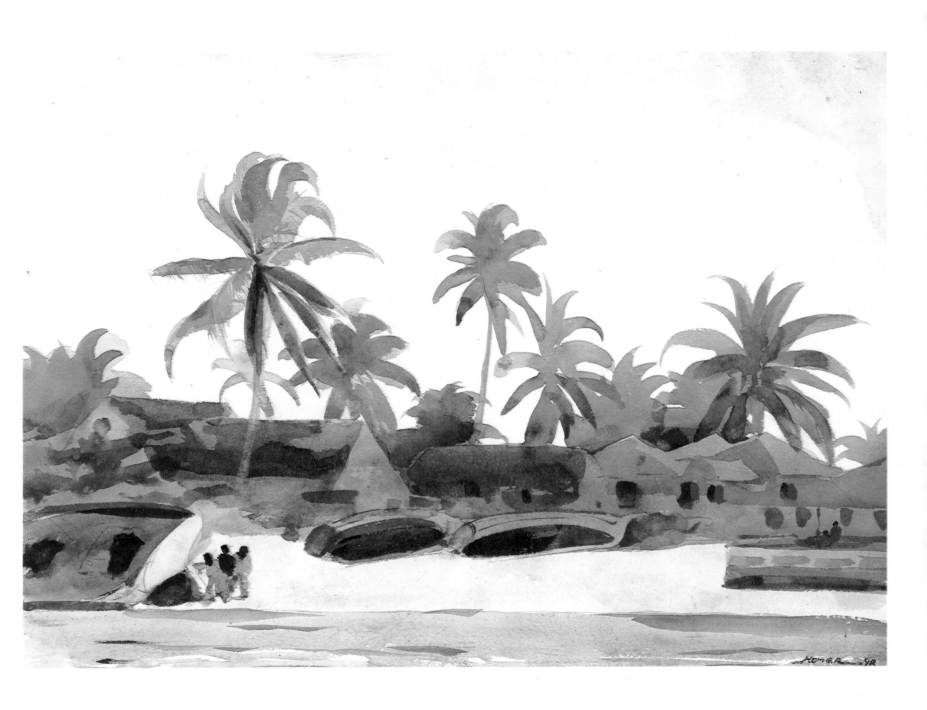

Plate 14

NASSAU, 1899

15" x 21³/₈" (38.1 x 54.3 cm.)
The Metropolitan Museum of Art
Amelia B. Lazarus Fund, 1910

Homer began the New Year at Nassau, in evident good spirts. What amused thoughts of his snow-covered studio at Prout's Neck must have passed through his mind, as he tackled the problem of transposing these azure waters to paper. The natives of Nassau and the Out Islands are consummate mariners; their boats are used for fishing a variety of sea creatures, including the famous conch—one of the delicacies of these islands. An anchorage of native sloops is not especially picturesque, except to the artist's eye. Homer found endless pleasure in the play of the transparent blue-green waters against the white hulls of the boats. The romance of colonial wars is also brought to mind by the inclusion of the ancient cannons, lying disused and rusted at the water's edge.

On this New Year's Day, Homer must have been full of immediate plans for pictures, for such subject matter—the native sailor and his sloop—became material for one of his most celebrated canvases, *The Gulf Stream* (The Metropolitan Museum of Art), finished by the end of 1899. Its mood of desolation and terror at sea is far removed from the idyllic charm of such a study as *Nassau*.

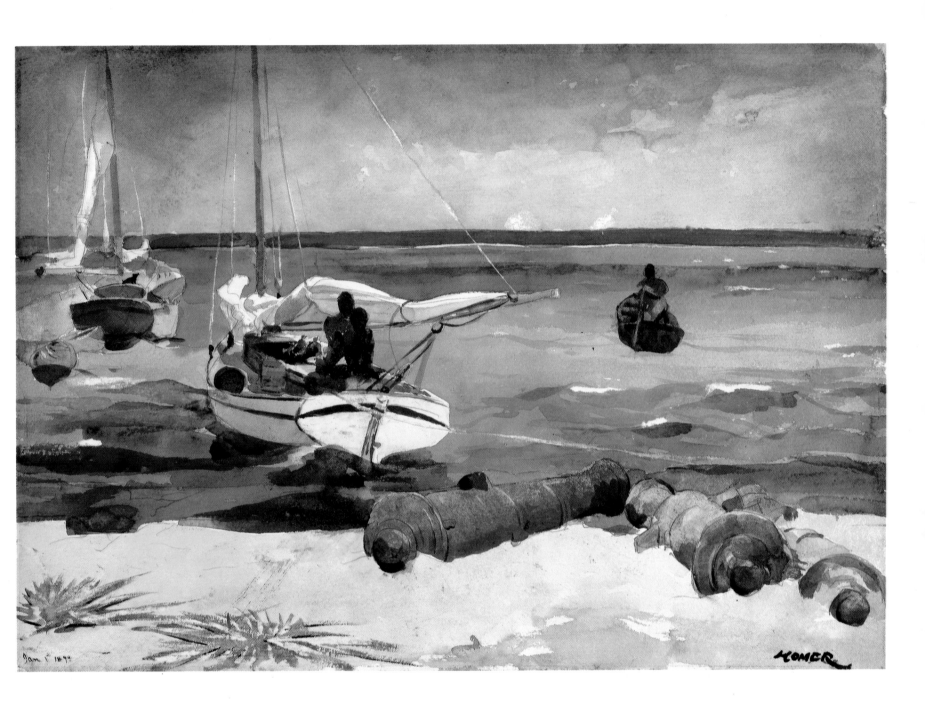
Jan 1 1899   HOMER

Plate 15

SHORE AND SURF, NASSAU, 1899

15" x 21⅜" (38.5 x 54.3 cm.)
The Metropolitan Museum of Art
Amelia B. Lazarus Fund, 1910

The Bahama Islands are composed largely of small coral cays. The waters are treacherous for mariners, since the approaches to natural harbors are often laced with coral reefs which lie hidden below the surface. When a sea is running, the reefs cause waves to break long before they arrive at the shore. Homer had probably seen this phenomenon along the Florida coast, as well as in the Bahamas. Here he records such a sight, taken from the vantage point of barnacle-covered rocks. As the running sea enters the lagoon, it leaps momentarily on the outer reef, creating a line of white, dancing waves. The inside of this, where the backwash of spent waves rolls in ascending and subsiding pyramids of foaming water, is described much as a turbulent pool. Across the face of the pool float skeins of ochre-colored seaweed. Homer's use of nearly irridescent emerald and blue is not an artistic exaggeration, but is rather an expression of uncannily accurate vision. Within the limitations of pigment, he has created in this watercolor an astonishingly close likeness of the sea at Nassau—not only in terms of color, but of movement and mood as well.

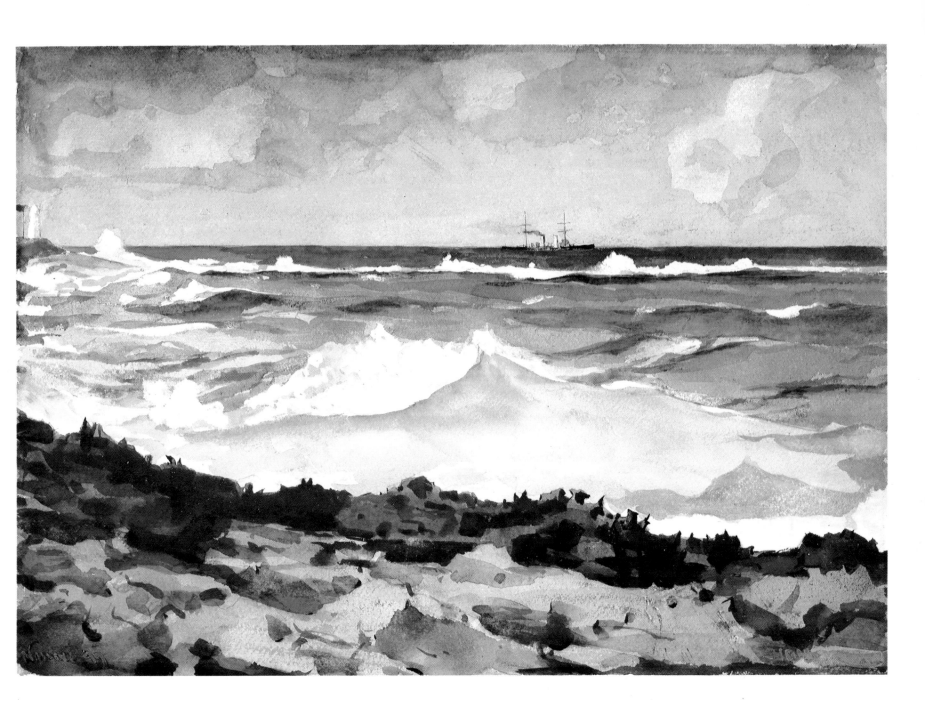

Plate 16

NATURAL BRIDGE, NASSAU, 1898

14½" x 21" (36.8 x 53.3 cm.)
The Metropolitan Museum of Art
Amelia B. Lazarus Fund, 1910

As much as Homer's studies of Bahamian walls would seem to indicate a playing with notions of occult balance, so this aerial view of the great natural bridge signals a release from the expected composition of a landscape view. A large portion of the paper is given only the slightest articulation, and Homer seems to enjoy letting stand that long, unbroken line of the horizon—against all conventional rules of good compositional form. As the eye draws near the bridge, the tempo quickens until, at last, all the accents of color erupt in the lower right corner in a nearly Fauve brilliance, dominated by the soldier's scarlet tunic. Such pictures tell much about an artist's capacity for creative invention. For Homer, it suggests that had he not been so convinced of the virtue of painting as closely as possible to nature, he might have extended his enormous capacity for invention beyond visual reality.

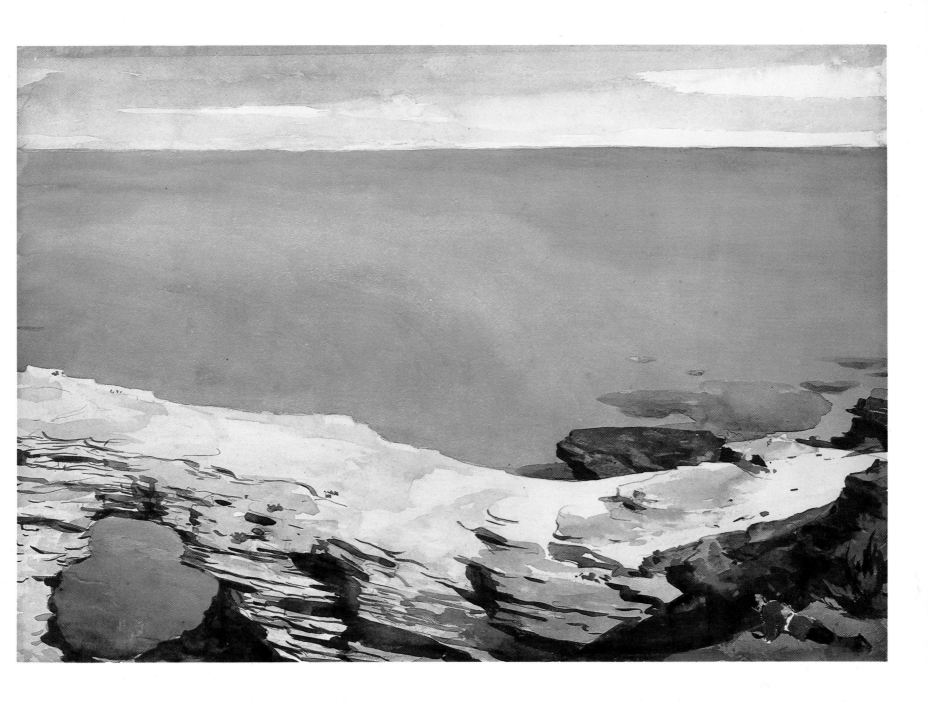

Plate 17

GLASS WINDOWS, BAHAMAS, ca. 1885

13¹⁵/₁₆″ x 20″ (35.4 x 50.8 cm.)
The Brooklyn Museum
Purchase Fund, 1911

Although this work is undated, it relates on the basis of its technique to dated examples such as *On the Way to Market, Bahamas.* One of the artist's Prout's Neck watercolors that was done some two years before *Glass Windows* makes use of a framing device within the composition itself which isolates a small section of the ocean beyond. In the Bahamas, Homer found that nature had prepared for his arrival; no rearrangement of rock formation was necessary to accomplish a re-creation of his Prout's Neck conceit.

The title of this Bahamian subject is the artist's own, which he took care to inscribe. The suggestion of a window formed by the arch of the natural bridge is apparent; the reference to "glass," less so. In studying the work, a possible explanation for the term may be deduced by observing that the sapphire clarity of the water meeting the horizon might be taken for a sash window open half way: the water is the "glass." But this is not a transcendentalist's visual pun; Homer is celebrating the light that bathes the rock and the sense of space and atmosphere that opens out onto a world of infinite distance.

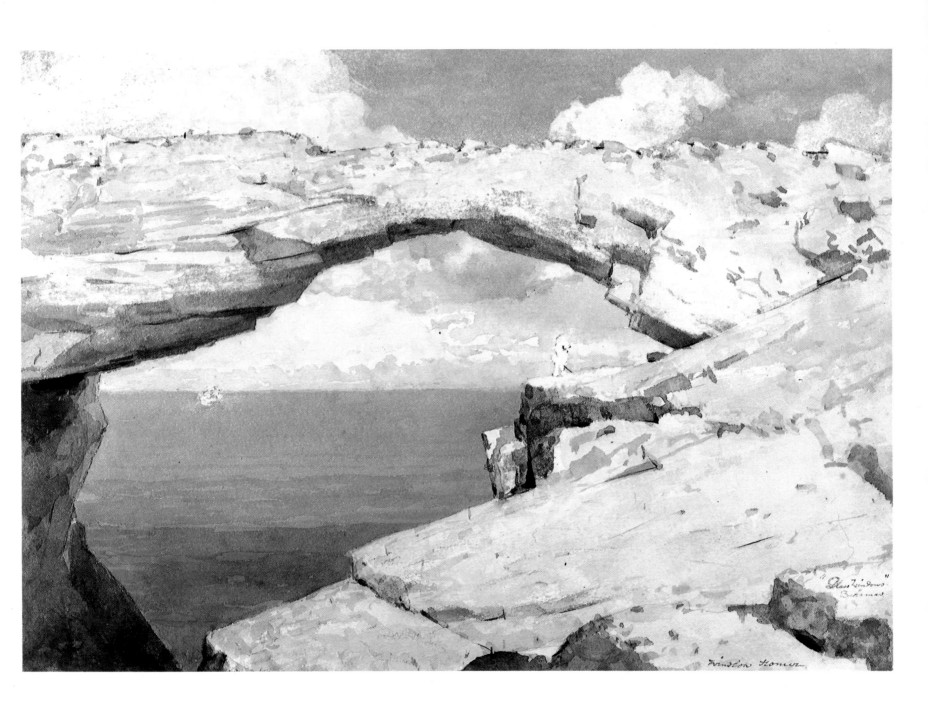

Plate 18

SLOOP, BERMUDA, 1899

15" x 21½" (38.1 x 54.6 cm.)
The Metropolitan Museum of Art
Amelia B. Lazarus Fund, 1910

With the completion of his monumental oil *The Gulf Stream,* based on his Bahamian experiences, Homer rewarded himself with a trip to Bermuda, in December of 1899. He had cause to feel important that year. Thomas Clarke, who had owned some of his best pictures, had put them up for sale the previous February; they had fetched record-breaking prices. Although Homer did not benefit financially, the sale—the most important one of its kind up to that time—enhanced his reputation enormously.

The Bermuda watercolors are freer and more lyrical in color than those of even a year before in the Bahamas. The sloop is set in a sapphire sea, above and beyond which a new drama of cloud formations sets an appropriately complementary background for the touches of pink in the swirling arabesque of the loosely furled sails. There is an ease of drawing and a certainty in the placement of each color passage that speaks eloquently of Homer's sense of personal well being.

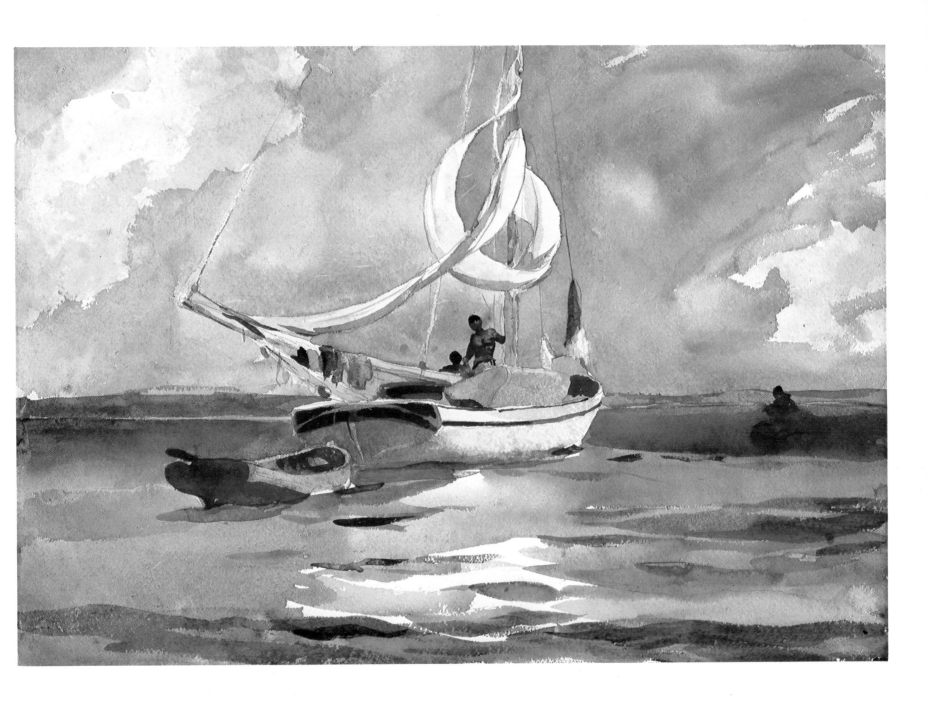

This subject, along with one other in the Brooklyn collection, has long been associated with Homer's Nassau period. Examination of both reveals that the houses represented are characteristic of those found on the island of Bermuda. *House and Trees* is probably an unfinished work, for the foreground, with its incomplete figures, appears to be merely a first wash which was never built upon. It is tempting to speculate about what the figures are intended to be doing. The color, Indian red, suggests newly turned earth. The figures of the children seem to be stalking on all fours some unseen object of their attentions. Homer has worked toward unification of color by introducing the same red into the trees, a practice which appears occasionally in his seascapes.

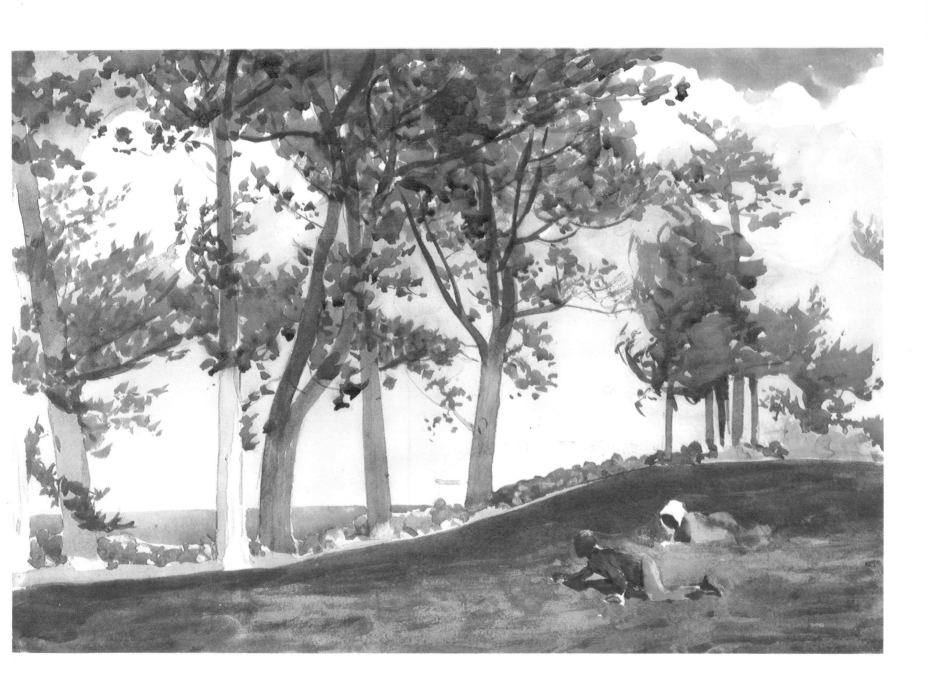

The richness of color noted in the watercolor, *The Sloop, Bermuda,* is shared by this warm and vibrant work. Formerly titled *Shore at Nassau,* its relationship to the Metropolitan subject, *Flower Garden and Bungalow, Bermuda,* is eminently clear in the comparison of the houses represented. Both show the terraced stone roofs typical of the local architecture of Bermuda. *Shore of Bermuda* is one of Homer's seemingly effortless compositions which reveal exceptionally careful planning. The picture is constructed to lead the eye inescapably to the small, brilliant color note at the center left. It is a work of opposing values, weights, and hues. In spite of his essentially flat application of intense blue and his sharp definition of the horizon line, Homer achieves a remarkable credibility for the distant ocean. The artist demonstrates the effectiveness of employing quite analogous color relationships, while creating an interestingly colorful picture.

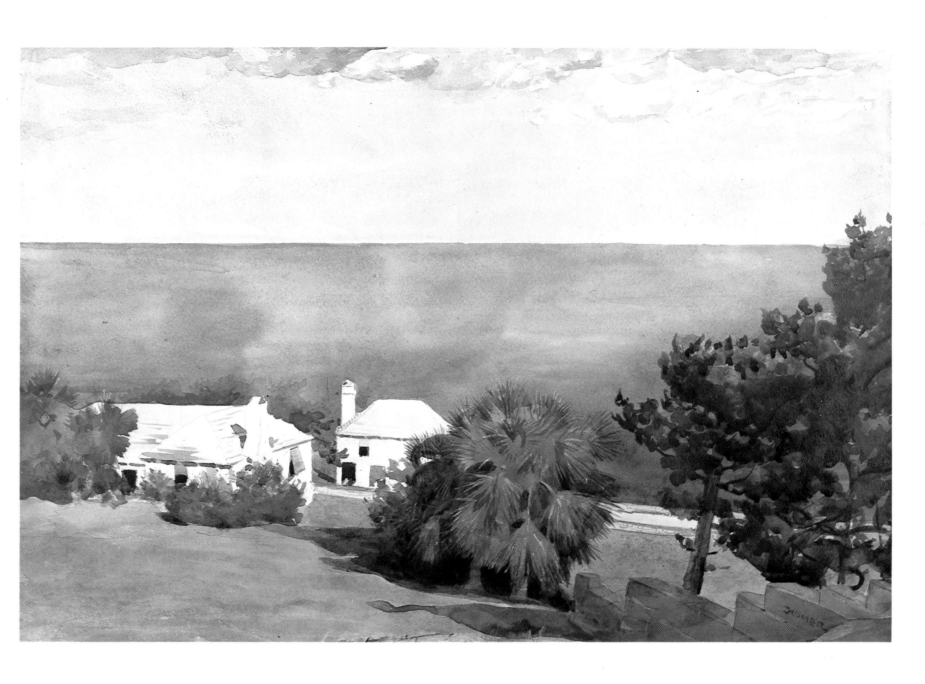

Plate 21

FLOWER GARDEN AND BUNGALOW, BERMUDA, 1899

14" x 21" (35.5 x 53.3 cm.)
The Metropolitan Museum of Art
Amelia B. Lazarus Fund, 1910

In keeping with his happy frame of mind that winter in Bermuda, Homer seems to have abandoned himself in this watercolor to a mood of rapturous color. Once asked if he did not agree that beauty is essentially abroad everywhere in nature, waiting to be seized by the artist, he replied: "Yes, but the rare thing is to find a painter who knows a good thing when he sees it! You must wait . . . patiently, until the exceptional, the wonderful effect or aspect comes." With this garden scene, one feels that Homer must have instantly recognized the exceptional.

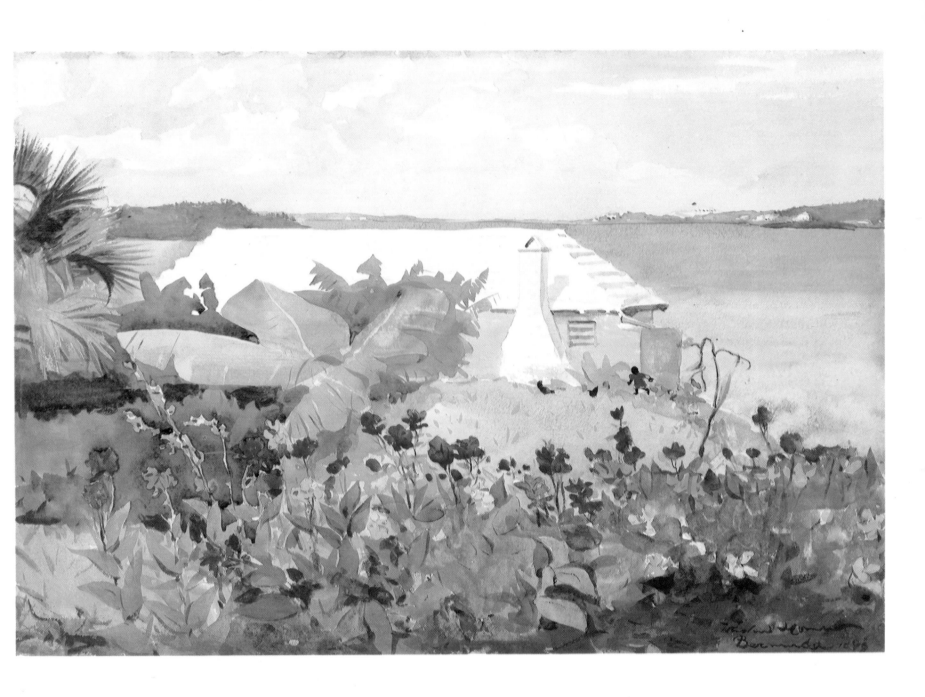

Plate 22

THE BOATMAN, 1891

13¾" x 20" (34.9 x 50.8 cm.)
The Brooklyn Museum
Bequest of Mrs. Charles S. Homer, Jr., 1938

Except for his Adirondack pictures, and a very few of the Maine subjects, Homer had little
recourse to employ models. His tropical—and even his Québec—watercolors concentrated
on the large view of nature, while the last oils from Maine exclude the human element
altogether. In the Adirondack subjects, however, there are two recurring characterizations:
the bearded old man and the youth. In most cases, these figures appear alone in the vast
mountain landscape. Beam points out in his book that Homer apparently had alternates for
the mountain men—doubles who would pose for Homer in his studio at Prout's Neck when
the artist was putting the finishing touches to a canvas begun in the mountains of New York.
The identity of these counterparts is known; they were brothers whom Homer had
befriended, John and Wiley Gatchell of Scarboro, Maine. The subject of *The Boatman* is
thought to be a young farm boy, Mike Flynn. He appears in several of Homer's most important Adirondack oils, including *Huntsman and Dogs* (Philadelphia Museum of Art) and
Hound and Hunter (National Gallery of Art, Washington). In *The Boatman*, he is shown
as the familiar young man rowing a skiff (probably on a lake near Minerva in Essex County).
The scene is suffused in tones of gray, and the figure in his boat seems suspended between
sky and water.

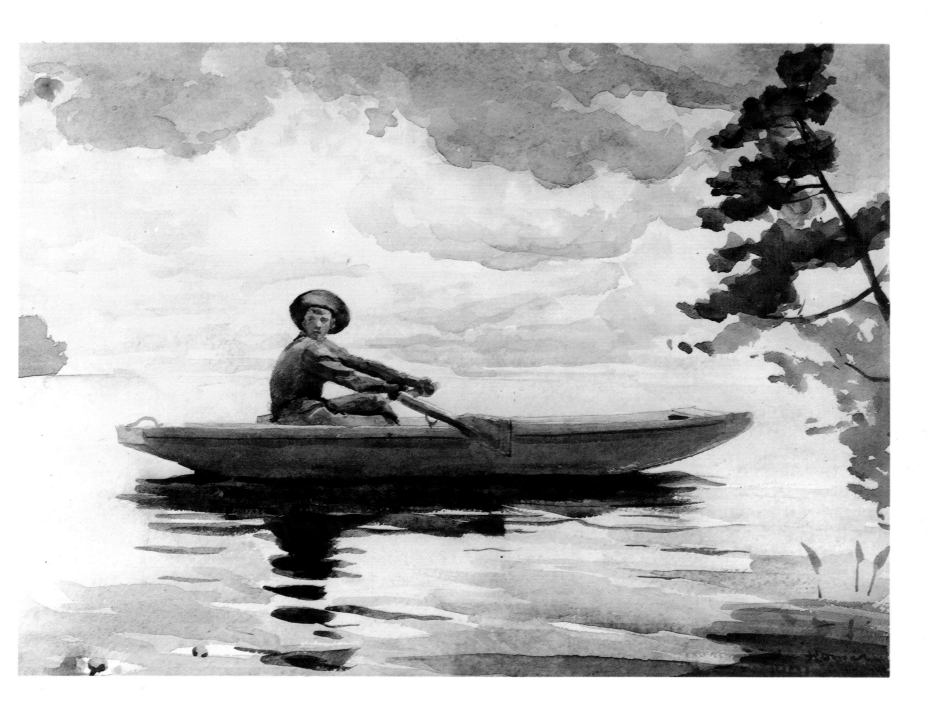

Plate 23

BEAR AND CANOE, 1895

13¹⁵/₁₆'' x 20'' (35.4 x 50.8 cm.)
The Brooklyn Museum
Purchase Fund, 1911

On his second trip to Québec, Homer was accompanied by his brother Charles. Homer did not hunt, but he was a fanatic about all kinds of fishing. In order to insure good fishing, he joined a club which operated an exclusive preserve on the shores of Lake Tourilli, about thirty miles northwest of Québec City. The trip in 1895, his second, proved to be something of an expedition, since Homer seems to have been determined to seek the even more remote fishing holes further north, in the area of Lake St. John. The bear subject is inscribed "Aug."—the first of the two months of his expedition into the north woods. It was probably inspired by an actual occurrence, but the exact circumstances are not recorded. The treatment, decidedly humorous, seems almost pure whimsy on Homer's part, except for the fact that he was working prodigiously and very likely wanted to include every aspect of his trip. Homer carried a small Kodak camera on this trip; and from 1895 on, it became as much a part of his equipment as his painting gear. Obviously, the bear did not stay in camp long enough to pose, but possibly Homer was able to photograph the creature as it dined on a choice part of the canoe's birchbark construction or on some spruce gum patching.

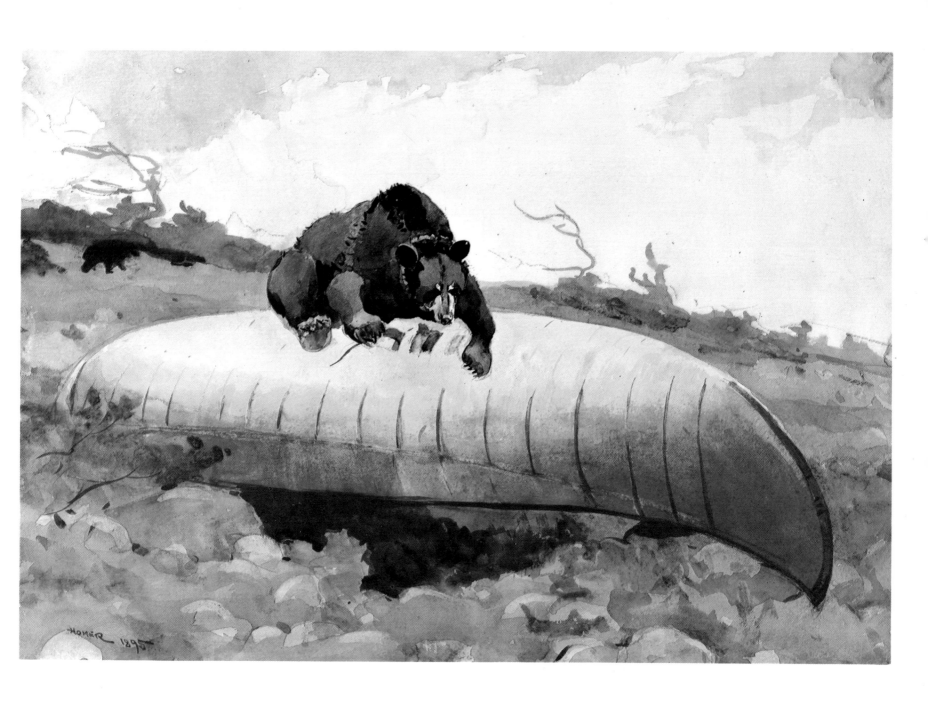

William Downes, Homer's first biographer, attended an exhibition of The Boston Art Club, where *The Pioneer* was first exhibited, and recorded his impressions of the watercolor in the margin of the show's catalogue: "Violent and crude, but pungent and powerful. Vivid light. Fresh and crisp. Cool bracing air . . . A rough bit of country." After periods of confinement in his studio at Prout's Neck, the Adirondacks provided Homer release for his searching eye and, additionally, the pleasures of his favorite pastime. He arrived there in June, 1900—the year he painted *The Pioneer*—and reported to his sister-in-law Martha, "The fishing is over here and I am sketching in watercolors." Goodrich observed that very few watercolors were actually produced; and in a succeeding trip to the Adirondacks, Homer did no work, contenting himself with the fishing.

Except for two months in 1908, when he was recuperating from a paralytic stroke, Homer never returned to these mountains; nor is there any evidence of new work based on Adirondack themes. *The Pioneer*, then, may be regarded as his last statement on the subject. There is an elegiac quality to this watercolor. Unlike his earlier pictures of mountain men who stand triumphantly atop their world, the human element in this subject seems to echo the forms of the few remaining trees of a forest that has nearly vanished under the axe. The late afternoon, with its mellow light casting long shadows across the land, contributes to a sense of finality. Perhaps this represented Homer's feeling about the encroachments of civilization upon a country whose wilderness he had known and loved in former years.

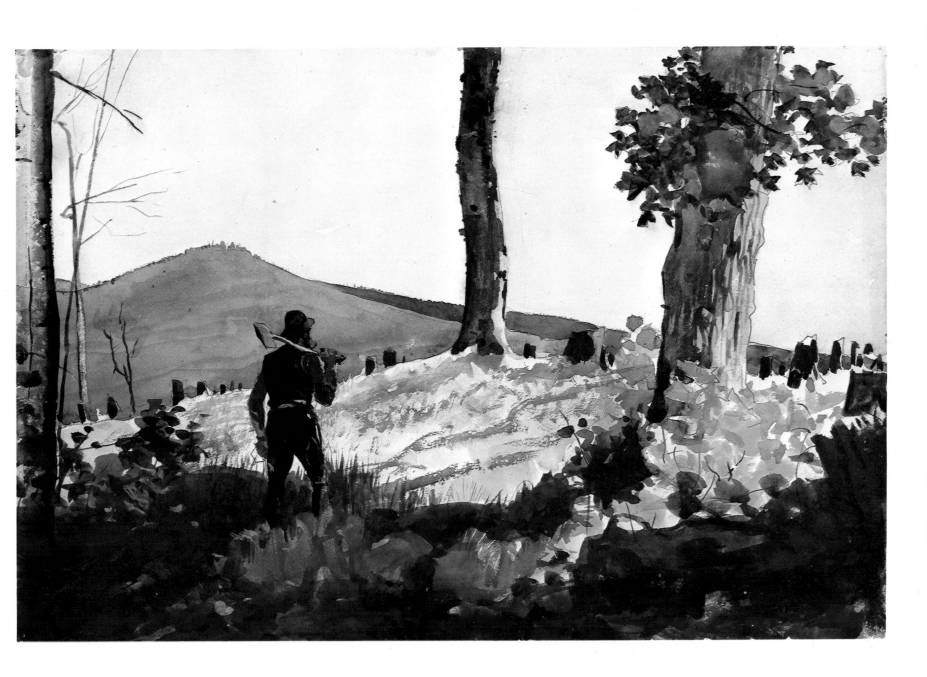

Plate 25

FISHING THE RAPIDS, SAGUENAY, 1902

13¹⁵/₁₆'' x 20⁵/₈'' (35.4 x 52.4 cm.)
The Brooklyn Museum
Purchase Fund, 1911

His initial trips to Québec in 1895 and 1897 must have whetted Homer's appetite for further exploration, but he did not return until August, 1902. He had departed Prout's Neck, sending a note to Knoedler, his dealer in New York, "*Work* now is in order with me!" Certainly, he had not slackened in his production of new paintings, nor were his efforts unrecognized. He had won a gold medal for *Summer Night* (Museé d'Art Moderne, Paris) at the 1900 Paris Exposition, as well as another gold medal for a group of watercolors shown the following year at the Pan American Exposition in Buffalo. Another consideration—his advancing age—must have prompted his concern for continued activity. His letters reveal that the Québec trip was undertaken as much for gathering ideas for paintings as it was for pleasure.

The upper Saguenay River, near its source at Lake John, drops swiftly toward the St. Lawrence River in a series of roaring rapids. *Fishing the Rapids* carries all of Homer's authority in handling the effects of turbulent water. Here he returned to the restricted palette of his Tynemouth watercolors, combining dull blues with passages of ochre, which he used to describe what rivermen call "white water." The slight coloration found in the churning rapids is set with great effect against the blueness of the total composition; for all its simplicity, the picture seems rich and full. On the distant mid-stream rock, a fisherman casts his line into the lower rapids. Homer recorded the action with consummate ease, describing the arc of the line by scratching the wet paper with the pointed end of his brush.

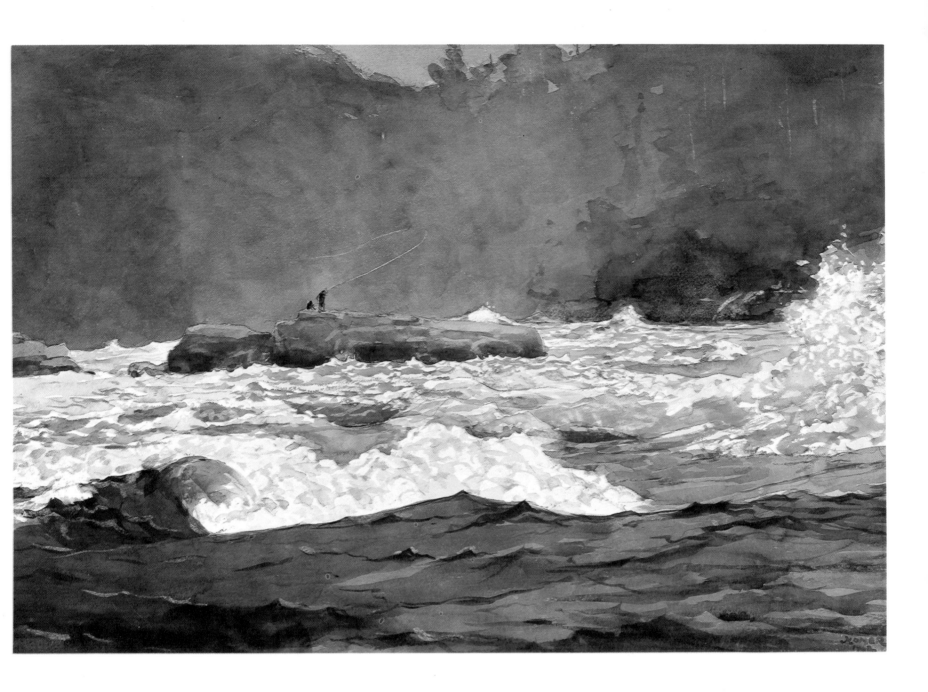

Plate 26

SHOOTING THE RAPIDS, 1902

13⅞″ x 21¾″ (35.2 x 55.2 cm.)
The Brooklyn Museum
Purchase Fund, 1911

In the woods of northern America, where rivers and lakes abound, travel is accomplished by canoe. Descending big rapids in a canoe is an exciting experience, one that challenges the skill of even the most experienced hand. Homer reacted to this excitement during his second trip to Québec, immortalizing on paper and canvas the era of the *Québecois* woodsman and his birchbark canoe. These works had a special importance in his career, as he commented in a letter to a dealer in Boston on two watercolors sent for exhibition: "I value them highly, as I could make a fine picture by combining the two in an oil painting."

Shooting the Rapids became the basis for the proposed oil painting, now in The Metropolitan Museum of Art. The oil, which remained unfinished at Homer's death, nevertheless indicates the excitement Homer wished to convey, for he sketched in the leaping white water of the rapids more powerfully than he had in the watercolor. Yet the watercolor remains a more accurate statement for, unlike the oil painting, it shows the canoe slipping quickly in the current, its course guided by hands sure of their task. Homer observed the postures and attitudes of his rivermen, noting how the man in the stern braces himself against the thwart and uses his paddle as a rudder, while the man in the bow reaches out with his paddle to help avoid a rock or to correct the course. Again, as in his marine subjects, Homer conveys with the utmost economy of means a sense of movement and energy in the water: no line or color is included that does not contribute to the impression of the profound truth of his observation.

72

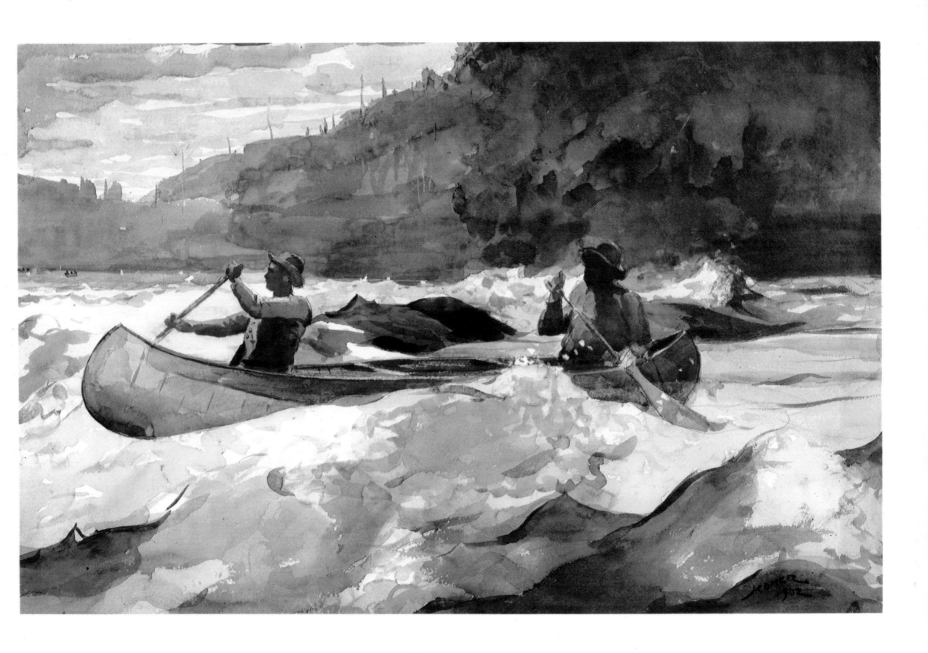

Plate 27

JUMPING TROUT, 1889

12⅜" x 19⅜" (31.4 x 49.3 cm.)
The Brooklyn Museum
Dick S. Ramsay Fund, 1941

Homer was an outdoor man all of his life and, while he spent much of his life among the mountains and rivers of North America, he never hunted animals. His few pictures of animals usually convey a kindly attitude about them. His enthusiasm for fishing, however, led him from Canada to Florida; but, again, he admired fish as objects of beauty—as much to be observed as enjoyed for the sport. He found particular rewards for the eye in the trout and *ouananiche*—Canadian landlocked salmon—of the north woods. These fish are famous for the powerful way they strike a lure and, when hooked, offer the angler a tenacious struggle. When landed and dead, their superb lateral coloration quickly fades; but observed alive, they are creatures of indescribable beauty.

Homer knew this; instead of painting his trout like a kind of still life, he chose the more demanding action picture. Against a dark background of deep browns and blue that suggest a shadowed woodland pool, Homer has contrasted the flashing, silvery body of the trout. Below the trout, the surface of the pond marks the point where the fish has erupted from the water in its pursuit of the lure. To the knowledgeable eye, Homer has shown the trout aiming not for the scarlet fly in the picture, but for the second—and invisible—lure at the end of the barely visible leader. The picture is composed in rich and subtle colors; the velvety background offers an appropriate foil for the resounding brilliance of the trout and the appealing accents of scarlet and pink. In its simplicity and the easy assurance of its draftsmanship, *Jumping Trout*, an Adirondacks picture, might have been painted by some oriental master of watercolor.

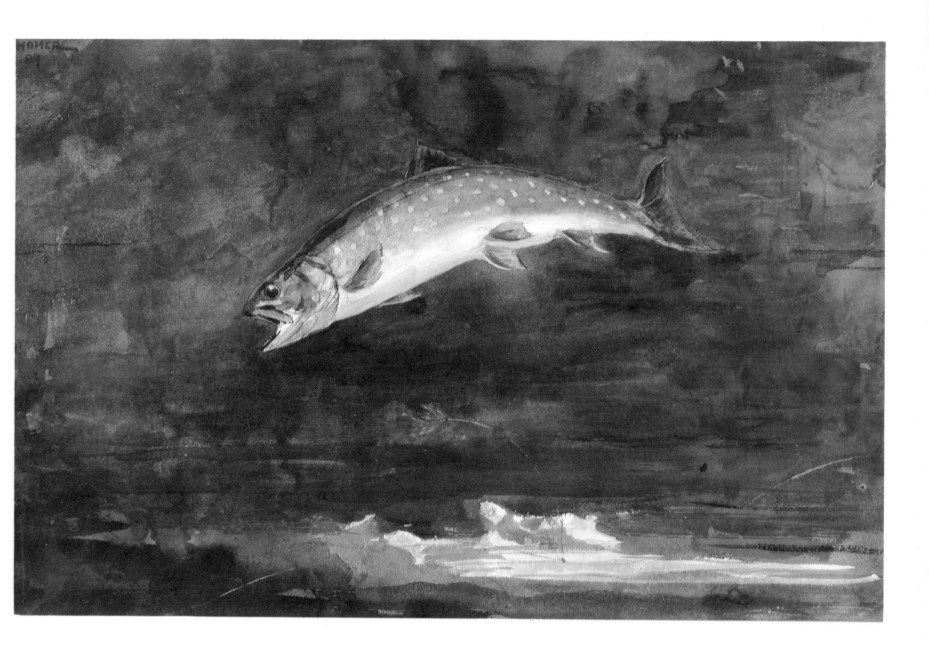

Plate 28

FISHING BOATS, KEY WEST, 1903

13⅝″ x 21½″ (34.6 x 53.3 cm.)
The Metropolitan Museum of Art
Amelia B. Lazarus Fund, 1910

Early in December of 1903, Homer boarded a steamer in New York bound for Florida, where he stayed the winter, seeking refuge from the discomforts of a northern winter. He wrote to his brother Arthur on the eve of departure, "I decided to go direct to Key West . . . I know the place quite well, and it's near the points in Florida that I wish to visit. I have an idea at present of doing some work, but do not know how long that will last. At any rate I will once more have a good feed of goat flesh and smoke some good cigars and catch some red snappers . . . ." Although he was garnering more gold medals at national exhibitions, they were being won for old pictures—his current production of paintings was nil.

In his sixty-seventh year, Homer was showing signs of slowing down. In Florida, where he undoubtedly dined on the snapper, he also made at least one watercolor of the channel bass, one of his favorite game fish. Presented with the reviving color of Florida and physically restored by its warm sun, Homer resumed working in earnest. The Key West fishing boat subjects rank among his most successful works in the watercolor medium. In comparison with similar pictures made in the Bahamas and Bermuda, the Key West paintings reveal a greatly increased fluency of technique. In *Fishing Boats*, Homer's placement and balance of contrasting masses seems at the point of perfection. Particularly in the vessel drenched in sunlight, he exhibits a virtuoso's mastery in the handling of the pure white paper, on which he controls every nuance of form by the justness of his drawing.

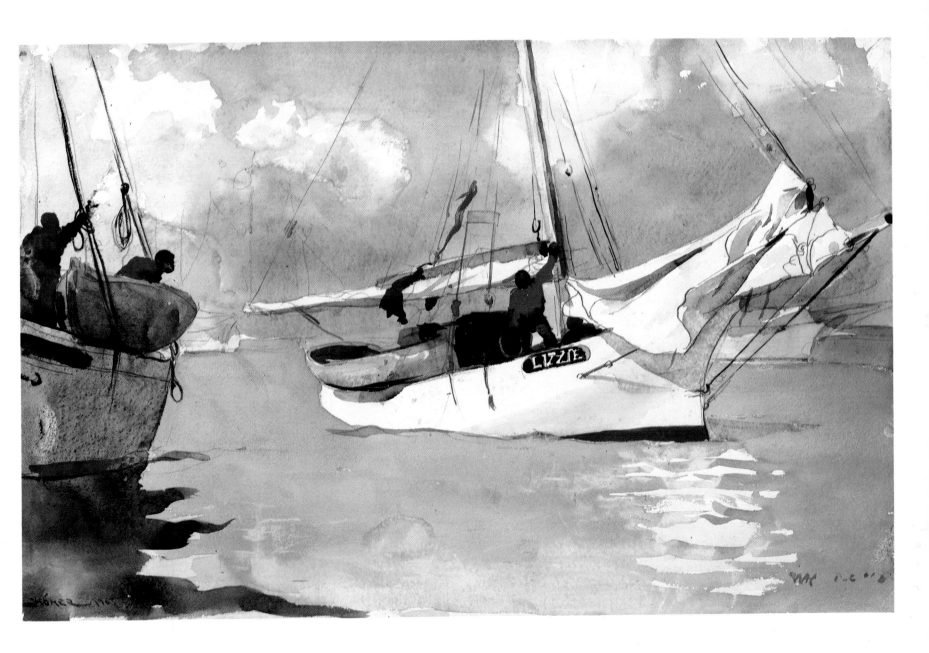

Plate 29

TAKING ON WET PROVISIONS, 1903

14" x 21¾" (35.5 x 55.2 cm.)
The Metropolitan Museum of Art
Amelia B. Lazarus Fund, 1910

Homer was at the very peak of his powers in the 1903 Florida marine subjects. His feeling for form and light seems to spring from the level of instinct although, to be sure, keen observation preceded the movements of his brush. There is a feeling of utter, joyous abandon in the act of painting these works which may be imparted to the old-fashioned humor of the picture's title—the "wet provisions" are barrels of rum.

Homer set himself a task of formidable difficulty: to create a feeling of form and weight in a subject illuminated directly from above and bathed on all sides in reflected light. The adjustment of his values is exact without being pedantic. All of the accumulated sensibility of his hand and eye is thrown with seeming effortlessness into this watercolor. The counterpoint of its color harmonies is audacious. The reds run the gamut from chocolate to scarlet; and the blues, from the palest tints to emerald and indigo. Yet by concentrating the reds as brief accents, the dominant blues are made to vibrate with a pellucid light. In such pictures, Homer shows himself a poet of color.

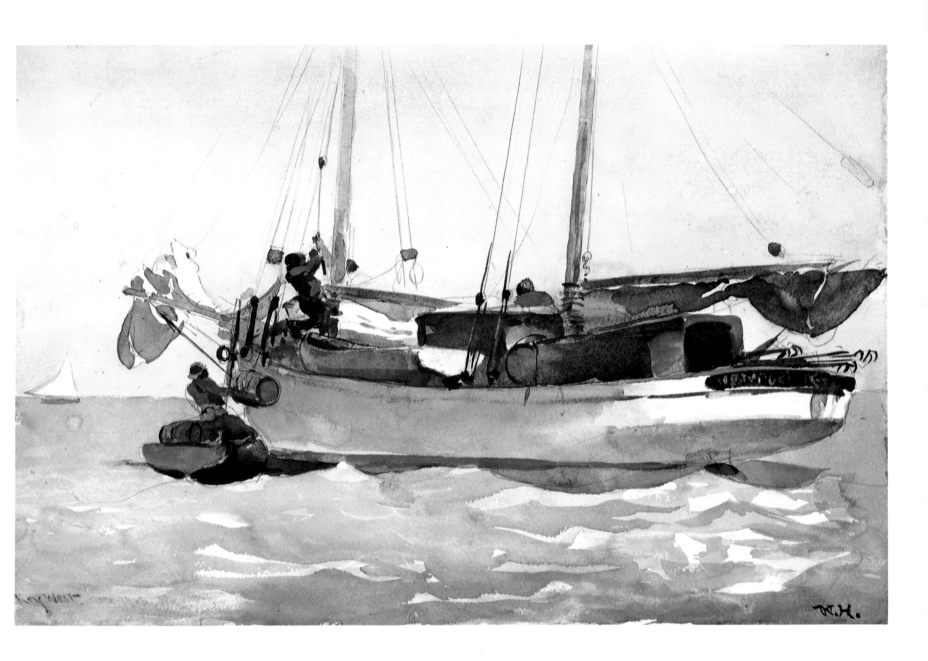

Plate 30

THE SHELL HEAP, 1904

19¹¹/₁₆″ x 14″ (50 x 35.5 cm.)
The Brooklyn Museum
Purchase Fund, 1911

Homer's various trips to Florida led him to Tampa and the Gulf Coast in 1886; to the St. John's River area in 1890; and then, following a few weeks at Key West, to Homosassa Springs early in 1904. He is reputed to have said that Homosassa had the best bass fishing in America. The sport offered him an excuse for embarking upon some of his freest improvisations in watercolor.

In *The Shell Heap*, only the slightest pencil notations support the washes of color. In this picture, Homer very nearly abandons line drawing in favor of the broader working of form by means of the loaded brush. Noticeable, too, are passages of daring color relationships, for example in the area of the embankment where pure black and white juxtapose slashes of red and ochre. The staccato grouping of gray palm trunks, with their accents of deep emerald at the left, suggests movement and life, helping to relieve the essentially static composition based on simple verticals and horizontals.

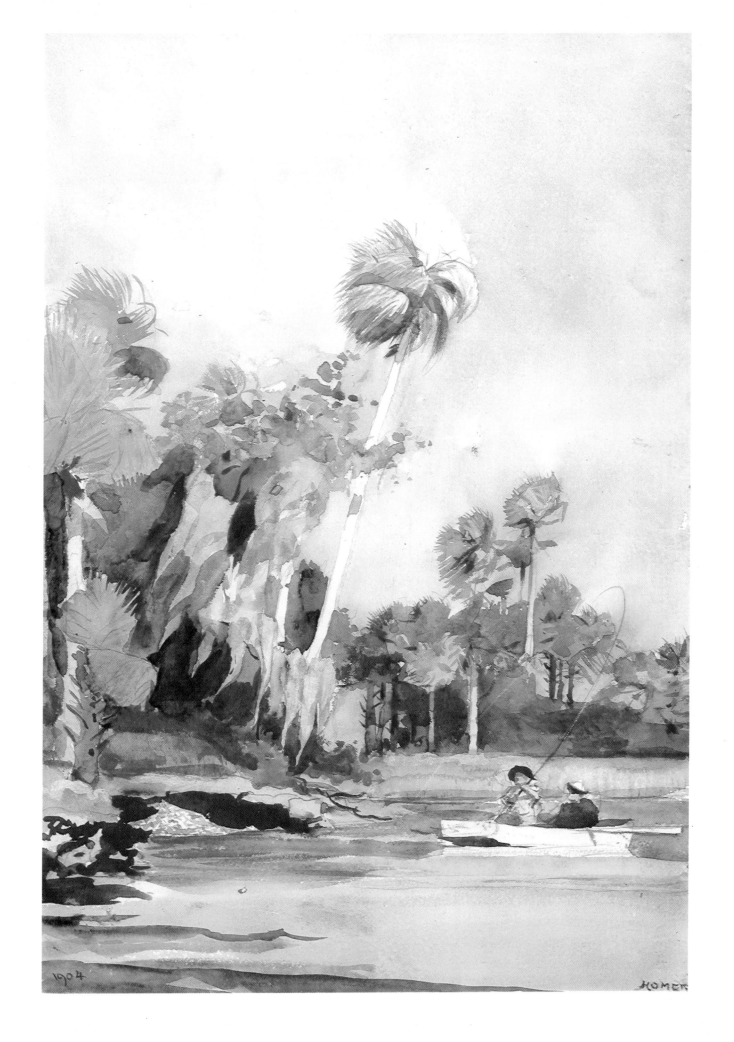

Plate 31

HOMOSASSA RIVER, 1904

19¾" x 14" (50.2 x 35.5 cm.)
The Brooklyn Museum
Purchase Fund, 1911

The weather in Florida is often unpredictable. Homer (even though he found the temperature too cold for painting watercolors during his stay in 1905) was able to catch a variety of its moods in his sketches. In contrast to *The Shell Heap*, with its golden-topped palms and the limpid light of its sky, *Homosassa River* reports on another kind of day—one that afforded him inspiration for working out subtle color harmonies. The general impression of this water-color is grayness; upon close examination, however, rich passages of color present themselves. The composition is based on blues and greens; but, as in all Homer's works, small secondary accents of bright color set off and define the principal color. In this case, the yellow oil skin of the fisherman predominates, and the subtle washes of magenta in the hanging Spanish moss add a certain richness to the deep blues and greens.

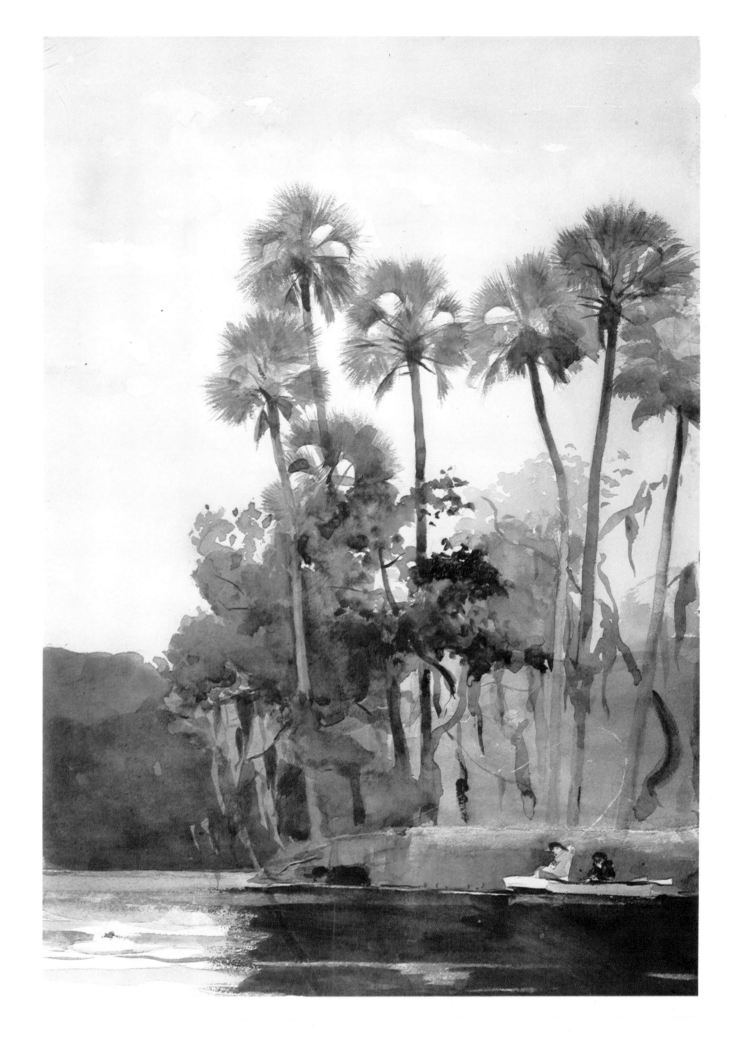

Plate 32

IN THE JUNGLE, FLORIDA, 1904

13⅞″ x 19⅝″ (34.9 x 49.8 cm.)
The Brooklyn Museum
Purchase Fund, 1911

The location of this scene may be central Florida, possibly the Everglades National Park. Its central element, a cougar climbing a palm tree trunk, is full of Homer's customary sentiment for wild animals (and in this case he leaned heavily in the direction of humor). Although the circumstances surrounding this work are not recorded, the comical aspect of the bellowing beast seems to insist upon an explanation. Since one of the synonyms for cougar is "catamount"—a favorite term among writers in the nineteenth century—this representation may be an obscure pun. Such historical detail seems like an irrelevant aside, when taken in the context of the scene. Homer has composed a cohesive whole out of the chaos of a swamp forest interior.

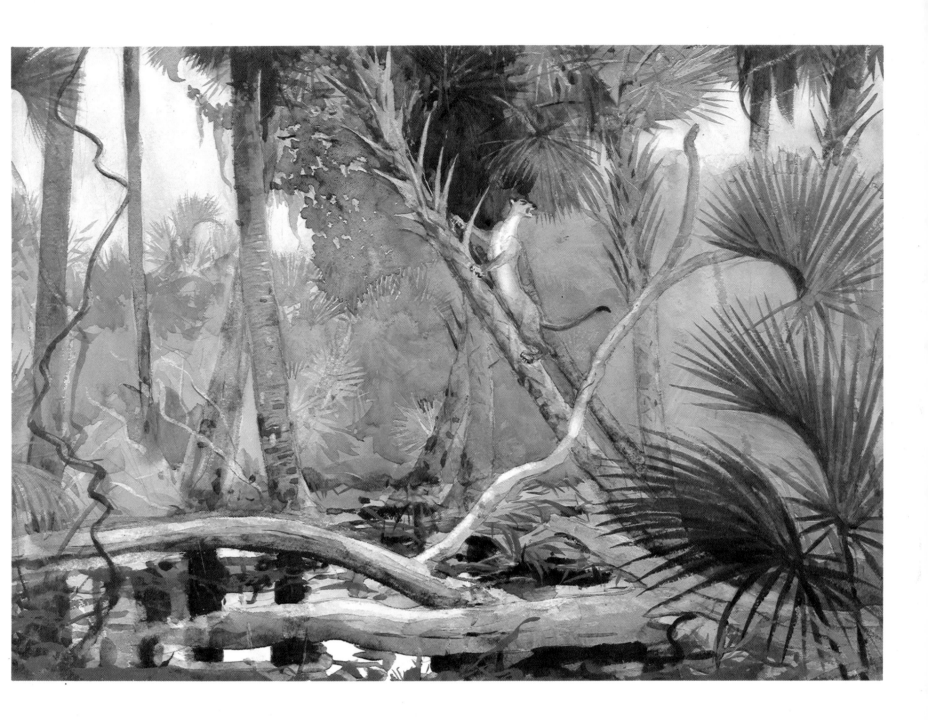

Edited by Judith A. Levy
Designed by James Craig
Composed in twelve point Bodoni by Phototype Systems, Inc.
Printed and bound in Japan by Dai Nippon Printing Company